Praise for Ginnah Howard.

Rope & Bone: A Novel in Stories

"Howard weaves together a collection of short stories to create this powerful novel about two very different women and the children upon whom their accidental sins are visited.... Spanning from 1946 to 1993, the book lays bare Del's and Carla's lives with quiet compassion, wit, and an unhurried anticipation. Stunning in its simplicity, Howard's lean prose belies the detail and richness of the characters she conveys." —*Publishers Weekly (Starred Review)*

"In the vivid, searching light that Howard sheds upon each woman's life in turn, we see the forces that pull them together and push them apart without judgment, without any oversimplified sense of angels and demons. Carla's life spins farther out of control, while Del strives to rein hers in; we come to love them both. …Howard's time-shifting Zen take on the perils and pleasures of loving rings very true. Families, friendships, catastrophes, achievements: life really is what happens when you're making other plans, and Howard excels at telling the truth about women who live on the hardscrabble edge."
—*Chronogram*

Night Navigation

"The strength of this story pulls Howard's readers along, unable to turn away from a fierce mother and son who are determined to negotiate the future." —*New York Times Book Review*

"Harrowing . . . Howard's strength, besides lapidary language, is the ability to build scenes around quotidian activities . . . Stark scenarios will be cathartic for readers who have dealt with them first hand, and profoundly cautionary for those who haven't."
—*Kirkus* (Starred Review)

Doing Time Outside

"Ginnah Howard guides us through a gritty America caught between a small-town bar, a church, and a jail cell. Through compassion for her characters and the buoyancy of her voice, Howard gives us a novel with a generous and intelligent heart." —Mermer Blakeslee, author of *When You Live by a River*

"Catskill's wordsmith Howard has a gift for the choice, mundane detail: the vinegar chips and Advil headaches and warmth of a dog's fur on a cold day. Her turf is the Upstate New York just outside of the weekender realm, and her people are fiercely smart and loving throughout their frustrations and misunderstandings. You start really, really wanting Rudy to make it, a topic around which Howard builds mind-bending suspense. It all comes together in a knockout ending—Howard's characters have grown and so have we. A beautiful read." —*Chronogram*

I'm Sick of This Already

At-Risk Learning in a High School Class

Ginnah Howard

I'm Sick of This Already: At-Risk Learning in a High School Class
© 2015 Ginnah Howard
www.GinnahHoward.com

All rights reserved. Reproduction without express permission from the author or publisher is prohibited.

Published by

Illume Writers & Artists
PO Box 86, Gilbertsville, NY 13776

Published in the United States of America

Author's mailing address:
Ginnah Howard, P.O. Box 149, Gilbertsville, New York 13776

ISBN 978-1517104115

Design by Jane Higgins
Cover photo by Ian Austin
Author photo by Rose Mackiewicz

Note: The names, as well as certain identifying details of people and places in this book, have been changed.

Preface

The winter after I retired from twenty-seven years of teaching high school English—mostly in a small town in upstate New York—I began writing a teacher-narrative about working with fifteen students in an Improvement of Language Skills (ILS) class that met daily during period 6B right before lunch. This class, made up of a mix of sophomores, juniors, and seniors, had elected to spend all three years in my ILS group rather than be in traditional English or the Resource Room. Using scenes of classroom activities and their written work, I gradually told about each of these students.

I don't ever remember having a story move forward so easily. Each day, during a month-long residency at an artist colony, I wrote from nine to five telling about our gains and losses throughout the year. It was like having a job. By the end of February I reached The End. *I'm Sick of This Already* became my farewell to 6B, my goodbye to teaching when almost every Sunday night for all those twenty-seven years, I was filled with a mix of anxiety and doubt that I could actually go in there the next morning to teach six classes, one of which was often "beyond me."

I sent the manuscript of *I'm Sick of This Already* to Heinemann, a well-respected publisher of books for educators. In a month or so I received a peer review from Heinemann that began with the word "Wow"—the opening paragraph of that review is on the back of this book. But the accompanying letter said that Heinemann seldom published teacher-narratives. If I would turn the manuscript into a "how to" book, with much more pedagogical thrust, they might be willing to publish it. I had no interest in doing that. I tried a few more educational presses—the same story. And so, I put the manuscript away in a box on my top shelf.

But I did keep on writing—publishing an Upstate trilogy: three novels which are described in the opening pages of this book and on my website: www.GinnahHoward.com

However, with the increasing concern these last few years about inequality in America—the "great divide," "equal opportunity, our national myth," the growth of an "underclass"—I thought again about my 6B students. I asked friends who are still teaching secondary English in rural schools, "Do you have students in your classes that are far below grade level?" "Yes" was their answer.

Why this is so is a subject for other books, but of the consequences there is little doubt: If a child doesn't learn to read and write by third grade, if day after day he or she can't do the work, complications accrue: inattention, acting out, feelings of failure, absence from school…Problems that reverberate through our whole society. In our hyper-media age, it is more vital than ever for students to develop the critical skills to recognize when they are being manipulated and lied to (and when they are not).

Though the classroom situation in this book is pre-Common Core, Wi-Fi, and Smart phones, teachers who have read the manuscript tell me that the story of 6B is still relevant. Moreover *I'm Sick of This Already* is a unique story since it deals with issues in a small rural town rather than the inner city.

So I took *I'm Sick of This Already* out of the box and read it again. I cried and laughed and remembered why I sometimes wished to see some of the 6B names on the Monday morning absence list. When I came to the final scene, I believed that this teacher and these 6B students sitting in that classroom watching *Great Expectations* had gotten somewhere.

I thought, "Now, that was an inspiring story." It was as though someone else had written it.

For my 2500 students
and all the lessons learned

*All that is valuable in human society depends upon
the opportunity for development accorded the individual.*

—Albert Einstein

I'm Sick of This Already

At-Risk Learning in a High School Class

I'm Sick of This Already
At-Risk Learning in a High School Class

Contents

FALL

1 Beginning
2 Stake
3 Stan
4 Joe
5 Vance
6 Allen

WINTER

7 How To
8 Neal
9 Cindy
10 Kathy
11 Patty

SPACE

12 Space
13 Props
14 Calvin
15 Robert
16 Mike
17 Joan
18 Rich

SPRING

19 Love
20 Lori
21 Vic
22 Jerry

ENDING

23 Lost
24 Balancing
25 Ending Big

Epilogue

Fall

1
Beginning

I sit up front next to Linda Nelson, a young fifth grade teacher who started last winter. We perch on the little pastel seats fastened to the long cafeteria tables. Linda is cutting out large red letters. She is full of right spirit; I lean into her aura. Across from her is the school librarian, Emma Lowe. She is seventy-six. A small, energetic woman who wears bright floral dresses and matching ballerina shoes. She has been the librarian for fifty-five years. She lives alone in a large Victorian house at the foot of School Hill and walks to work every morning, winding her way up through the cemetery.

The cafeteria bulges with laughter. Most of the tables are full. About a hundred of us in all: K-12 teachers, administrators, custodians, bus drivers, secretarial staff. Frank Davis, the new superintendent (another new superintendent), has taken his place by the overhead projector. He is young, in his late thirties, and he looks eager. He's red-cheeked and a little round. He is smiling. He wants us to become still, without having to make any authoritative gestures. The art of beginning any class: velvet. Some teachers, like the students who choose the back row the first day, keep on talking. They don't hop to.

This new superintendent grew up in Stanton and several of the teachers had him in class. Of the three top candidates, the teachers on the selection committee ranked him third. But now that he's been hired, we wish him well. We hope he is able, even talented. We know what a drain it can be on us all if he is not. We will wait and see.

Now Mr. Davis glances at the clock, but decides to wait a little longer. He chats with the President of the Board, Mary Norton, a woman disliked by many teachers after acrimonious and long contract negotiations; where things said are still not forgotten. She and her husband run a dairy farm. She is attractive, her bold chiffon scarf draping a smart dress. She has an MBA from Cornell. She has a younger child with special needs who not that long ago would have been called retarded. Mary Norton and her husband home-school their older high school daughter because they feel it better serves her educational potential. Nothing personal, she assured us as part of her last year's first day welcome. I admire her courage to stand before the group and talk as she will again today. Like trying to refloat in a class gone thick with animosity.

Emma Lowe leans across the table and smiles at us. She says she is glad to be back. Linda says she is too. This is my twenty-sixth year of teaching. Today is my 53rd birthday. This is my next to last year. I am not glad to be back, but I'm not dreading it.

If the first day of school in-service seems real, I usually sit in the front and pay attention. The exact opposite of what I did as a high school student; then I read a novel in my lap and never spoke. This is my chance to make up for what I might have missed in that hazy last row. My chance to be model. At the very least, this sitting for hours listening is a good reminder of what students must endure, because no matter how positive I am, always by the second in-service session I am wanting to slip off to the bathroom, to stand looking out the window as long as I dare.

Frank Davis smiles again. Far-reaching. The time has come. He steps to the overhead and turns it on. He welcomes us. He thanks the custodians for their fine work in getting the buildings ready, and we all join him in this, for the halls glow with wax, the desks and bathrooms are free of graffiti. We appreciate such a shiny start, such concrete gifts. Mary Norton welcomes us and expresses the board's hope for a good year. She smiles. She is brief. Her audience is impassive.

Frank Davis shows us transparencies on two topics which he says will be our major concerns over the next few years: student outcomes and shared decision-making. It's hard to keep believing in these overhead projections in a district that has had nine different principals and eight superintendents in the twenty years I've been in this system. This kind of turnover produces a faculty that pretty much fends for itself, a group resistant to the yet-another K-12 curricular overhaul, knowing the reams of goals and objectives inseminated during the last administration lie stillborn on some district office bookcase.

Really though, what I am most wanting to do the first day is to go to my room and in its still blankness to imagine the students entering, with us getting off to just the right start, so the rest of the year will slowly unfold from that chrysalis, the veins of our limp wings filling, to hover over word after word, the gift that is our language.

As soon as they are available, right after the morning session, I always pick up my first day packet: class lists, plan-book, first aid kit, a box of Kleenex. A weighty black loose-leaf marked, *Teacher Handbook,* a miscellany, including everything everyone should do and shouldn't. I always open my class list folder with excitement and fear. Most of the givens for the year are in it: class load and individual class size, number of preparations, number of periods you teach in a row, what kinds of students you have in last period classes, number of hard-core problems—combinations in any one class and in total. This is the lot you have been cast.

Some years I slip into my room, sit down, breathe deeply and fan the class lists open like a hand of five card draw and I'm already light. But today I stand at the main office counter and spread the sheets wide. A quick take on the weather ahead: the prevalent winds, the possible storms. What provisions must be stowed for the crossing.

HOMEROOM: 20 seniors, the same group I've had since ninth grade. "Home" is not how I do it. It's where I take attendance, maintain quiet during the pledge, the taped alma mater, the announcements. Where I pass out and collect communiqués. I've never mastered the art of "being here now" at the same time I collate, write on the board, assemble the materials needed for the six classes ahead. Or the art of feeling easy in a room full of adolescent oscillation and no structured plan.

FIRST PERIOD: Improvement of Language Skills (ILS: a class for students with reading and writing problems who are unlikely to succeed in the regular English curriculum. Students have the option to elect this program for three years if it's working.) There are eleven students on my list: four seniors, three juniors, four sophomores. Five of them were in my ILS classes last year. Matt Wallace again, the third year in a row, but he's come a long way. He used to be hiding under my desk at the beginning of the period. It's a real plus to have students with language problems first thing in the morning. They aren't bored yet. (Or are still too sleepy to resist.) My guess is this class will be okay.

SECOND PERIOD: English 12. Only ten students. Placid. Clear. I wish there were a few more, some promise of minor disturbance. I know them all from my tenth grade classes a few years back. No strong readers or writers, but a few enthusiastic learners. Dale Henderson, a boy whose journals spoke with an openness rare in tenth grade boys. One of those students everyone likes: an athlete, a yearbook editor, vice-president of his class.

THIRD PERIOD: Reading and Writing Lab. Six ninth graders and three tenth. Two of them from my first period class. I always have trouble staying pumped up to keep the labs real. What is needed is high energy to help these students believe that the deep, long-term language problems can, over time, be lessened. They would prefer to color their Global Studies maps and fill in Life Science blanks. They are resistant to actually reading and actually writing. In a few months I usually wear down. I slip into an unwritten agreement: If they work quietly, with me available to help them find answers to the homework questions, I won't push them to learn. Do better this year, I tell myself.

FOURTH PERIOD: English 10. Eighteen students. Another small class. For the past few years we've had the advantage of smaller groups. Way down from the class loads of one hundred and twenty-five to one hundred and fifty of earlier years. An overall drop in school population—the closing of several of the area's few industries. I will be replaced by a half-time teacher when I retire next year. I check the list of sophomores. I don't know many of them. Only one infamous person.

FIFTH PERIOD: Planning. A chance to regroup. Go to the bathroom. Do a few vocab quizzes at my desk while I eat my crackers and cheese. I seldom go to the faculty lounge. Sometimes this can be isolating, but I have such a desire for silence after four straight classes. And often I want to lower the stacks of papers that need to be returned to students tomorrow. If I work through lunch, I won't have as much homework. Recently I estimated that in my twenty-six years of teaching I have processed/evaluated/corrected at least 300,000 papers. This is the part of teaching I long most to be free of.

SIX B: Another ILS class. I scan the names. Here it is: THE class. The one I will take home with me. The one that will make my neck ache. The one I will learn the most from. I count. Seventeen students. I count them again. ILS classes are usually kept to twelve so there is time to give individual help.

One of the middle school teachers reads the 6B list over my shoulder. "Good luck," she says. "You'll need it." I don't respond. I'm already manning the control towers, searching for units that will maintain security, my sanity, until the class gets the rhythm.

I head for the guidance office still reading the list. Twelve boys, five girls, nine are "special ed" meaning they have severe learning problems and are not in any regular academic classes, but are "mainstreamed" into any classes that might work for them. Eleven of the seventeen I know from my ILS classes last year. I wonder why Victor Gantz is in both ILS and English 10. Especially why ILS when I know he's a good reader.

The guidance office is jumping. There are already several people waiting outside of Joe Marsh's door. I take a chair and begin to imagine a seating chart that will minimize the damage. The number of students who have behavioral problems is beyond my personal talent. Right away I see that there is not enough space in my classroom, not enough seats to put distance between all of the potential troublers, not enough docile buffer students to totally surround each of the difficult ones. Stop it, I tell myself. Let each kid have a fresh start. But my over-voice says, Be ready.

I glance at the list for my last remaining class:

SEVENTH PERIOD: another English 10. Twenty-eight. Large, but full of students who do well in school. Believers. Students whose talents, whose parents' values, match up with what the school defines as successful: high grades, punctuality and good attendance, cooperative behavior, goals for higher education.

And my eighth period is marked PLANNING. Ahhh! Not to teach English the last period of the day is a gift, for by then we are all dulled by the barrage of fluorescence and words.

Finally Joe is free and I'm less anxious. He swings around in his swivel chair, in a tiny office lined by file cabinets and so stacked with boxes, with crisscrossed piles on every plane, I know that within days of working in this space, I would go mad. A cheerful man who married late, with two infants and a wife who teaches full-time. I'm fascinated by those so little in need of order.

"Why so many in the afternoon ILS classes?" I ask him.

It turns out that the courses most of the students take at the area vocational center (BOCES) are only offered in the morning this year: body work, auto mechanics, security officer, construction and large equipment, food service, childcare. This puts seventeen in the afternoon class.

I ask about Victor Gantz. Joe says Victor has got to pick up an English credit since he didn't go to school all those months he was in Florida last year. That he'd rather do ILS than repeat English 9. It's a good trade-off for maybe keeping him in school.

"What's the story on Allen Lange?" I want to know.

Allen's here on contract. If he's uncooperative and disruptive, he's to return to a self-contained class at BOCES. ILS is his only mainstream class. He'll be in the resource room the rest of the afternoon.

"Allen Lange in a class of seventeen; not the most auspicious beginning," I say.

Allen has been identified as a "person in need of supervision": truancy, refusal to accept basic classroom structure, inability to stay focused, occasional outbursts of violent behavior (kicking a boy in the head in sixth grade.)

Joe promises me that if someone isn't working out, we'll deal with it. I know he means this. Since most of the ILS students are not being programmed to get local diplomas, but rather have Individual Educational Plans (IEPs), four English credits are not required. All manner of alternatives are available.

At last I find myself in my room. I walk its edges, run my fingers along the shelves of books that fill the side wall: the easy to read winners in the best spots, all the new paperbacks standing half-opened along the top. I sit at my big desk in the back of the room, its surface still empty and cool.

This is a good room. Large and light and alive with huge student murals above the blackboards and shelves, all done as class projects under another teacher before I inherited this room. I remember for a whole year she managed her classes around large ladders and buckets of paint, the floor a litter of drop cloths and rags. I would have found it hard to be with that much chaos for that long, but I'm glad to be the recipient of the fifteen-foot green and red dragon flying across the front, *Macbeth's* witches around their cauldron on one side wall, and a sphinx rising from the mist on the other.

I open and close the big cupboards by the door, feel the pleasure of ample supplies: chalk and scissors and glue, the stacks of construction and composition paper. I slide the two new erasers along the trough below the blankness of the blackboard and then write my name in my best teacher cursive. Playing school.

From the big windows on the back wall I look down on the town, its one main street with the single traffic light controlling its one intersection, the National Bank, the Victory Market, Bates Funeral Home, the municipal building that houses the fire station and town clerk. The rest of Main lined with other small town needs: Nina's Pizza, Valley Hardware, The Stanton Gazette, Debbie Dean's Dance Studio, Blanchard's Drugs, and just beyond the corner, heading toward the river, the post office, the library, D.L. Harper's Feed.

The day is so clear I can see beyond the business area to where the houses begin. At either end of town there used to be gas stations, both run by former students who showed up dutifully each day for English, their hands still bearing witness to late nights with carburetors; students who approached paragraphs with the same steady perseverance they must have used in loosening a nut on an old car; students you always knew were going to be okay. The garages have recently been replaced by a Jiffy Stop and a liquor store.

I register that the clock tower on the municipal building has the same wrong time it had when I started teaching here twenty years ago: 9:06. I remember my first view of this school, high on terraced hills with concrete walks and steps leading down to a long lawn at the center of town, a lawn banked by a big cemetery on one side and the First Baptist Church on the other. I remember liking that it looked like a school, three stories of solid tan bricks, its many windows and entries large and sure. A WPA project, like the junior high I'd gone to in West Virginia. After a long stint of sixties relativity, perhaps I found its solidity reassuring. I had been teaching in a liberal high school near Madison, Wisconsin, where students had an open campus, could opt for credit or no-credit rather than grades, could help design their own individual curricula.

The beginning of that summer, my husband and our two young sons had moved to this valley to live on fifteen acres of my husband's family's land, to build a stone house following some of the Nearings' dictates. *Whole Earth Catalog*, "back to the land" romantics. I had left my six years of teaching in the Midwest exhausted, determined to get out of the classroom, sick of it all. Then, a week before the start of the school year, our money disappearing at an alarming rate, I began calling to see if there were any jobs. Two days before the opening of school I found myself with six classes, two of them seventh grades with thirty-eight students in each—wall-to-wall energy.

Most of the educational experiments of the sixties simply never found their way to this rural district. At first I was appalled by the hall passes and "no gum chewing" rules—such a presence of unabashed authority—but it was here that I began to learn what it meant to deal with large class after large class of students who expected *me* to be clear about why we were here, clear about limits. I found myself glad to return to teaching Dickens and Twain. I realized how weary I was of student-chosen projects on abortion and the legalization of marijuana. That I hoped never again to teach another thematic unit that included *Anthem, Animal Farm,* and *Johnny Got His Gun.* Though I had learned a lot from the educational reforms of the sixties, as I began teaching in this more traditional school, I found that student choice, flexible grouping, and self-evaluation were all possible within the more structured classroom. Within a curriculum that had a rich literature base.

Now it's the beginning of another year. Outside in the hall I hear teachers locking up for the day, calling cheery jokes to each other about the coming onslaught. I sit on the stool at the podium. Can I really come in here tomorrow and do this? I make up a seating chart for 6B. I put Victor Gantz a little off by himself. Maybe it can be set up so that he can work independently. I move Allen's seat three or four times. Up front so I can keep connecting with him and help him when he gets stuck or further back where I won't tend to overreact to his every move? I outline my plans for sixth period, positive, but firm; plans with no free time.

    I fold my hands and fix on the hemlock that parallels the flagpole. I pray to the gods.

2
Stake

The bell rings. I stand by the door, tread water and breathe, ready to greet 6B by name. Ready to declare the boundaries and the willingness to grant space…IF. Their English folders are placed on their assigned desks.

Most classes, that first day back, are subdued, a combination of best behavior and shock. But not 6B. They surge into the room complaining:

"I'm hungry."

"I'm sick of this already."

"I hate English."

"How was your summer? What's up?" I say, trying to connect with each one. Trying not to go down.

"Your folders are on your desks," I repeat to each new wave as three or four more crash in.

Neal, with a shaved head. Joe, wearing three earrings, one a silver cross. Vance, in dark glasses and a heavy navy jacket, the same one he wore the few days he attended last year. Cindy, many pounds heavier. Joan, as a blond. Calvin, earnest as ever, his new pencil case fastened carefully to his new five-subject notebook. I am surprised, but glad, to see Kathy here instead of in regular English 12 as planned. A new boy. I say, "You must be Sam? I'm Mrs. Howard." He nods nervously and hands me a change-of-schedule slip. He'll move to morning ILS tomorrow. Good. One less mass of atoms whirling about in this 20 by 20 foot space sixth period. I point him toward a seat.

Several more students roll in.

"Why can't we sit where we want?"

"I'm not sitting by him," several say.

They mean Vance.

"Everyone sit where I've placed your folder today. If you have a real problem with where you are, see me after class and maybe we can make a few adjustments."

Ugh, my first mistake: Vance's neighbors.

"I want to speak to you," Robert says softly.

"Me first," Lori shouts and moves her seat as far away from Vance as she can.

I quietly ask Jerry to remove his baseball hat. He thinks my request over for a few seconds and then complies.

Hats in school are an issue in my district. For some teachers, a hat in a public building represents disrespect and the general crumbling of our culture. Hats are not symbolic for me and asking someone to take one off feels like an invasion of his space. However, after a two-hour faculty hat discussion last spring, mine was the only dissenting vote. I have made the decision to comply as well.

Jerry twirls his black cap around and around on the end of his finger.

Finally, finally everyone is seated. I take roll silently, trying to catch each eye.

SEATING CHART — 6B (12:15 to 12:57)

Row 1	Row 2	Row 3	Row 4	Row 5	Row 6
Victor		*Patty*	*Cindy*		*Lori*
	Sean	*Joan*	*Sam*	*Vance*	*Robert*
		Calvin	*Beth*	*Joe*	*Jerry*
Neal	*Rich*	*Mike*		*Allen*	

All present except Beth, who has gone back to live with her real mother they tell me. I add in Kathy.

"Well, here we are once again," I say. I can't quite bring off a "how glad I am to see you" so I go for irony instead, "and I know how happy you are to be back."

Moans, groans, laughter.

"Like I'm happy to go to the dentist," Mike says.

I note that Mike is wearing the latest fashion: baggy shorts that extend to just below the knee, and I guess are worn very far down on the hips beneath his long oversized sweatshirt. I often wonder how designers feel about their fellow-humans.

"First, let me just outline the routine we'll be following at the beginning. Most of you are used to this set up. We're going to start with journal writing..."

"I hate journal writing," Patty mutters.

"And reading a book together."

"Can't we do something different?" Joe asks. "Like poetry."

"Poetry," a chorus, with grimaces.

I roll my head gently. When my neck aches, I know the Tao flows elsewhere. "We'll do other things once we get started, but I think you'll like this book..."

"What book?"

"It's called *Cool World*."

"Cool," someone says.

"We'll start it tomorrow and I'll tell you all about it then, but first I want to explain how the class will be organized, then I want you to write a little, and finally to go over some of the ... rules."

I know that's too many words at once, but I can't stop myself from filling up the space. Jerry has his head down on his desk, his hat over his eyes, feigning light snoring. Allen is squeaking his sneakers on the parquet. His red hair and freckles, a continual neon-flashing on my periphery. I drift over close to Jerry and stare at Allen's feet. Jerry sits up; Allen stops.

I move to the list I've written on the board. Only about half the class bothers to turn and look at the words as I point to them:

Class Reading and Writing Unit (4 Weeks)
1. Journal Writing
2. Up and down the row "talk" on questions of interest
3. Read Cool World *out loud — teacher & as play*
4. Listening quizzes
5. Rough draft revisions and final copies based on journals
No assigned homework for the 1st. Unit

I explain a little about each item. Since most of the class have done similar units with me before, I try to be brief enough to keep moving, but detailed enough so the five students new to ILS will get the idea. They greet each explanation with protests: I'm not reading out loud; I'm not talking in front of the class; this is dumb. There's occasional grudging interest, especially about each day drawing from a box an anonymous student-question to use for writing and talking.

"All right, now I want everyone to write a five-minute journal today. You can use the paper in your folder if you don't have any." My attempt to anticipate everything.

Moans. Several I-haven't-got-anything-to-write-with. I hand out scrubby pencils from a cup I have ready. Some teachers never hand out anything. Bringing what you need is your responsibility, they say. I agree and admire their tough love.

"Put a full heading on the paper."

"You're going to make us work today," Stan says.

I want to glance at the clock, but I don't. I point to the heading I've already written on the board.

Name   *Free Writing Journal#1*
ILS (6B)   *September 9*

"Please use this basic heading all year." I give this directive matter-of-factly, as though I believe I will not still be saying these same words in January.

Mike, Stan, and Jerry do not raise their borrowed pencils, but the rest are concentrating, looking back and forth at the board as they copy.

When they are all done, I tell them, "The main thing when you write a journal is to try to find topics that interest you." I stop and scan their faces; I see that only a few are really "here." But I press on, "Maybe true stories about things that have happened to you like times you were mad or . . . Or you could tell about the first time you went hunting . . ." I hear my voice, its energy drained, weighted by the force of their indifference. Survivor panic jolts me: Day 1. Such torpor will not do.

I move in closer, start down the side of the room, pass within touching distance of Jerry and Robert. Neal and Allen turn. Front row seats have already made them wary; like Shane, they'd prefer to cover their backs. I cross the rear of the room, along the windows, head toward the far corner and Victor Gantz. Everyone but Vance shifts a little to keep me in view.

Back in front I survey their faces again, "What if I was to call on you right now and ask you to say one thing that really interests you?" The room pulses with adrenaline. If I could catch each face on film, measure their heart beats now . . . "What if I asked you to tell about one time you were scared?" And with that I stop short and command, "All right now, write for five minutes. Try not to stop. Don't worry about spelling. Write about anything. Get going!"

Calvin and Kathy raise their pens dutifully. Joan's bright blond head bends down and she is off and flying. And so is Joe, his body kind of swaying in rhythm to his hand as it moves across his page. An idea comes to Cindy. About half of them have started. But the rest stare at me, kind of push their bodies around. Dig in. Vic, Stan, Neal, Allen, and Patty all make it clear they're not buying it.

I do glance at the clock. Twenty-seven minutes to go.

Half the class is writing. Half the class is not writing. The optimism-pessimism game I will play all year? I move up and down the aisles. Encourage Vance and Jerry. I decide it was a mistake not to list a few specific suggestions. Having worked with eleven of them previously has lulled me into assumption. I realize that these first few days, weeks, months may be like starting over. Breaking through that resistance born of fear and habit.

"I don't like writing about myself," Victor calls out. "That's not anybody's business."

I travel in his direction, say quietly, "You don't have to write about yourself, Victor."

"Vic," he says. Loud and clear.

It wonder how Victor Gantz's 6B behavior will compare to his performance in the English 10 class which is loaded with students who want to excel. Though this is the first time I've worked with Vic, I've heard him spoken of in the faculty room with puzzled affection—a bright boy who's hard to engage.

I try again. "You can write anything you want to." I keep my voice steady, a cool match for their opposition.

"*Anything*," Neal says, rolling his eyes.

I see that he has his jean jacket pulled up almost to his ears. "Anything," I repeat.

"I don't want to write about *any* thing," Stan says.

"Remember, whatever you write is confidential. And if you write something one day that you don't want me to read, you just show me the paper so that I can give you credit, but you don't have to turn it in."

"So why bother writing it?" Patty asks. Her hands, with their bright red nails flutter up—just further proof of the nonsense that goes on within these walls, they say.

"Because it's good just to practice every day. To see that you have lots of things to tell about. To use some parts of the journals later as raw material for rewriting."

"We have to write it twice?" Stan says.

Such saboteurs. I check the clock again. "Tell how you feel about being back at school. Describe this room. Tell what you did this summer. But write."

Damn it, write.

Stan starts.

Normally I would do a journal also—to model the process, to create stuff I can share, to show that knock-out paragraphs do not flow from my fingers—but today I don't feel comfortable enough to let go of the class; don't dare to look down.

Now all but Allen and Mike and Jerry and Vic are writing. I ask Allen quietly what he's interested in? He tells me, Nothing. I ask him, What do you do in your spare time? He says, Nothing. I hand him a folder full of motorcycle and car and sports pictures and say maybe he will get an idea from one of these. Vic is turned away, his black leather jacket a shield, his arm blocking his page; maybe writing. Stan has stopped and is looking around trying to hook onto something. Jerry has his head back down and Mike has written two words on his paper and he is off in a dream. 12:43. I urge Stan with a smile and the wiggling of my fingers to continue writing. Surprisingly he does.

I wait for as many more minutes as I can get away with, silently cheering on those who look up. Joe is reading his over, crossing out and adding.

Robert waves his hand, his eyes through his thick glasses, indignant. "Mrs. Howard, it's been way more than five minutes," he announces.

"Nine," Lori says.

I still want to review a few basic rules, to spell out consequences.

First day is the best time to do that. Before the first incident occurs.

"All right, just finish up your last sentence. You can go on with the same journal tomorrow if you want to."

Kathy, Joan, and Cindy are still writing. I see they're all near the bottoms of their papers.

"Would anyone like to share what you wrote or just tell about your topic?"

"No way."

"Not me."

Several turn their paper face down and place their elbows firmly on top of it. I wait another half minute, but most of their bodies say, Don't call on me.

"As time goes on, you'll probably feel more comfortable. Just like last year. All right pass . . ."

"I'll do mine," Joe says.

We lean his way in surprise. He smiles and raises his paper with a flourish and then he begins to read with a sure voice, pausing in just the right places: "My Time in Texas. I looked down over the hill. The sound of dogs echoed in my head. My eyes focus . . . focused on the mountain lion. My blood ran cold. I saw the fear in the dogs' eyes as the lion tore into their bodies. The cry of the lion as the battle was done. The dogs laid dead all around the dominant one as they cried in pain and joy. The beast ran to the big rock cliff and howled in vain. The End. By Joe Tyler."

"Whooa, you wrote that in nine minutes," Patty says.

Joe smiles again. The room is still with admiration.

"Thank you, Joe." I want to place a large gold star on his heart. "Anyone else?" I begin to collect the papers.

"I don't want to turn mine in," Vic says. "Too personal."

I have him just show me the paper from where he's sitting. He has written about a fourth of a page. I tell him that's okay, but to be sure to keep the paper, that some of the best later work can begin with private journals. A flick of his shoulder advises me to save such speeches. I collect the rest. There's a lot of random motion in the room.

"Now we only have a few more minutes. I want to go over several ground rules."

"I'm starving," Jerry says.

I am too. Something tells me to wait until tomorrow, but I hate to begin tomorrow with rules. I speed on.

"Don't forget to place your folders in the 6B box as you leave class." I point to the front table. "Also it's important that you not disrupt what we're doing—that you don't keep the class from working."

I notice Stan is not paying attention. He's watching something on the floor.

"If you're disruptive, I will speak to you quietly about it. If the behavior continues, you will be sent to Mr. Booker's and you will return here with your lunch the next period."

I see that Joan is also watching the floor and Stan is laughing.

"If you continue to have a problem, your parents will be notified and you will be removed permanently from the class and given some alternate . . ." I walk over to Stan's row. He is poking a large brown beetle with his borrowed pencil.

"Stan," I say.

He picks up the bug and sets it on his folder. "Almost time to go," he tells me. The bright green of his new flannel shirt vibrates.

I turn to look at the clock. In that half-second he is out of his seat and walking to the front of the room, his huge work boots clomping. Feet that predict a much taller man in the near future.

"Stan," I say again, starting his way.

"Just putting my folder in the box like you said." He slides the beetle onto the folder table. We watch its hard shell body move this way and that down the wood.

"Stan," I say, my voice rising, "what did I just tell you about disruption." *What-did-I-just-tell-you* is always a signal they've got you on the ropes.

"Oh," he says, "sorry." Then he leans down, squashes the bug beneath his folder and scrapes it off into the trash.

"Yuwwww," several say, their lips turned down.

The bell rings. Stan drops his folder into the 6B box and slips out. The rest crowd through the door.

I follow, ready to catch Stan for a few private words. But there's not a glitter of green either way.

3
Stan

At the 2:55 bell the halls fill with the slamming of lockers, shouts, the stampede to make the buses. Joy—they are free at last. I linger at my desk. If I stay for just forty-five minutes or so I can probably get through everything that needs to be done by tomorrow.

I purposely choose Stan's journal as my first after-school paper. Begin with the most problematic and move on from there:

> *Jurnal*
> *9/9*
> *I get cows eveday and I put them and the stale. I fedd them hay and then I chaos them outside in to the pacess so they can eat grass then I go Back to the bran I fedd calfes, milk, and water and hay at night I fedd them gand and clean them.*

I find my left hand clinched in a hunk of my hair. Eleven years of reading and writing and this is how far we've gotten. I drag a student chair over to my desk and put my feet up. I am exhausted. The getting-back-in-the-traces after the stillness of summer, days that began with a good book in bed while I ate real bagels.

Tim Burns, a fellow English teacher who's been here even longer than me, passes my door and glances in. A half a minute later he reappears: He has registered me disabled on the side of the road.

"That bad?" he says.

"Stan Sadowski," I tell him.

"Oh." His smile is compassionate.

I appreciate that he does not offer some first day cheer.

"Go home," he tells me.

I know he's right. I get up and push all the piles of papers into my book bag.

"Take a long walk," he says at the head of the stairs.

I follow him outside. Only a few cars still around.

"Play the *New World Symphony.* Crank it right up." Tim gets in his car. I notice he has no briefcase, no books. He smiles and waves as he backs around to make the turn. Seeing me still standing there, immobile, he rolls down his window and calls across the lot, "*Mash* reruns."

He knows this is a time for directive counsel. When he sees I have finally gotten in the car and turned on the engine, he signals and disappears down School Hill.

I do switch on the radio, but I am still beset: Stan . . . Stan . . . Stan. I increase the volume. What to do about Stan? Should I let his first day bug-squashing go without rebuttal? Just start fresh tomorrow. I switch to the news. Or will Stan, the class, read that as the loss of round one? Give an inch, take a mile.

I do go for a walk. I do listen to Dvorak. Hawkeye and Hot Lips steady me while I set up my plan book. I reread Stan's journal and see beyond the errors: how hard he works, how skilled he is. All of this helps, keeps me from calling in sick for Day 2 of the 183 to go.

The next morning, when I make the turn up the hill, I decide: I'll catch Stan during my fifth period break, after the BOCES kids get back, just as he's headed for the library. Emma Lowe is charged with their containment for the ten or fifteen minutes before the beginning of 6B.

The morning goes well. The first period ILS class is pleased with *The Skating Rink,* asking questions, able to identify with Tucker's shame about his stutter. Matt Wallace waits until we finish the chapter before he signs out for the bathroom. The second period seniors are going to be a pleasure. We are starting with Tobias Wolff's *This Boy's Life*. All of them seem into it; Dale Henderson especially. He talks candidly about his father's violence when his dad had been drinking and that sets the tone for open discussion. Dale confesses he has never really read a whole book, cover to cover; several others nod in agreement. They laugh about all the phony book reports. But knowing what they've missed, how sad.

Third period lab and the fourth period tenth grade make me feel like it's good to be here, that our time together is going to be fruitful. In this mood of optimism, I am in the right spirit to talk to Stan. A feeling of easiness is not one of my main strengths. I often think such a center of calm is the single most important teacher quality and especially in dealing with troubled students, particularly a student who expects to be hassled, who can sense tense authority like a dog can smell fear. Easiness and approaching Stan one-on-one—no audience, less need to save face—though not guaranteeing receptivity, at least makes it a possibility.

At 11:55, about the time the BOCES bus usually pulls in, I take my position by the door. I breathe and wait.

I heard about Stan long before he appeared in my remedial reading lab last year. How his mother brought him and his brother one night in a taxi all the way from Jersey, deposited them on the porch of their father's farm house and sped away. How he was caught smoking in the bathroom in second grade. Stan had been in and out of special BOCES classes for children with behavioral problems since he was ten. He is now sixteen.

Sometimes last year, in the reading lab, when I could work with Stan individually, he would put forth concentrated effort. He chose a Hardy Boys mystery. He said, I want to learn all about the law because the last time my dad and I went to court, I couldn't understand half those big words Judge Meyers was saying.

We agreed that I would read one page out loud, with him following along by moving a card down the print; then he would read a paragraph or two, and I'd pick it up again when he got tired. He showed good understanding of what I read to him, but when he read, he soon lost meaning because he would never stop to try to figure out a word or even to let me supply it when he hesitated. Instead he careened down the page, filling in any old word that started with the same letter. Still, some sessions he would stay with it for as long as fifteen minutes. I kept telling him that if he would just continue, over time, he would see improvement. The days he worked well, he could "play around" the rest of the period on a computer program he borrowed from his Agriculture teacher.

In the lab last year I never could get him to do any writing, beyond one sentence every now and then under threat. And he would not work alone. Whenever I tried to spend time with one of the eight other students in the lab, he would engage in disruption: calling out, roving around bothering others, throwing things. Or sabotage: dismantling the desk screw by screw, ripping off the tips of the magic markers. He *would* have my attention.

One day at the end of the first semester in the lab, I told him to return to his assigned seat. He wouldn't. He insisted on sitting next to someone who was trying to read. Finally, I wrote out a pass and told him to go to Mr. Booker's, a "time-out" room. When he refused, I said that if necessary, I would have the principal come up and escort him. Stan continued to balk. At last I picked up the receiver to call the office. At that point he started toward me, with a sweet, chilling smile. He said, Put down that phone. He was removed from the lab for the rest of the year.

Stan does the work of a man on his father's dairy farm. He's able to drive any vehicle on the place, to repair the broken tractor, the malfunctioning milking machine. He is a good looking boy who often smells of the barn. When he's not engaged in sabotage or pushing the buttons of whomever is in charge, he's likable and honest about his modus operandi: I only act like this in school because I am bored and frustrated; at home I work hard and am responsible. Yesterday's bug incident is classic Stan behavior.

Stan is almost never absent; his father wants him to learn to read. His father, an immigrant from Poland, cannot read or write. All of his father's property is in Stan's name because of some kind of litigation.

His father's neighbors are full of lamentation. Collapsing barns, rusting trailers on makeshift foundations, and piles of refuse, blight the rural scene. The road by their place is almost blocked by disabled vehicles: tilting hay wagons, stalled cars, partially dismantled farm machinery. Chickens and geese make random crossings, car-chasing dogs appear from nowhere (one of our math teachers tells of having his bumper guards ripped by these marauders), and cows wander beyond poorly mended fences to stamp through another teacher's lawn several times a month. When this teacher tells of these incidents, his face drains of color, the muscles of his jaw harden. This has been going on for years, his dream of serenity deferred. I once asked him, Why don't you sell and buy another country place. And let them win? he said.

Stan lives in one of the rusting trailers with one of the hired men, a place without water or electricity. His father and his girlfriend live in the falling-down house.

Finally I hear the BOCES kids entering the building. I affect a happen-to-be-here-looking-at-the-folders non-pounce pose. It's important to catch Stan before he gets to the library. Culling him from the group in there would invite bravado. I've already let Emma know he'll be with me for a few minutes.

Here they come. I don't have a speech prepared—may the right words emerge.

Joe, the 6B poet, is the first BOCES student to make his way upstairs. He waves and then stops by the open door of the Economics class to blow a kiss to his girlfriend.

Stan's voice echoes up the stairwell. I register the intensity of its energy: 7 as in one notch below raucous. Adrenaline laps up some of my calm. Then Stan, wearing that same bright shirt, bounds into sight, two steps at a time. He sees me and grins.

"Stan. I was hoping to meet up with you for a few minutes before class. And here you are." I am smiling, friendly. And in his moment of not quite knowing what's up, I herd him through my door, toward a front desk. Corralled before Evasive Action kicks in.

"I'm wanting to get a few minutes to talk to each of my students individually, find out what you feel like you need to work on most this year." I open my mouth and these are the words that come out.

"What do you mean?" he asks suspiciously.

"Well, you know, like last year you wanted to read the Hardy Boys books so you could learn lawyer-language, what do you most feel you've got to learn this year?"

He thinks for a minute. Then he pulls a wad of papers from his back pocket. He unfolds several wrinkled, dim, dittoed worksheets.

"I need help with my welding homework for tomorrow. The teacher said if we don't do the worksheet pretests, he won't let us do the welds the next day."

I look over the first sheet. "I don't know any of the answers, but ..."

"Oh, I'll know the answers," he says, "once I know what the questions are."

I glance at the clock. "We've got ten minutes before class. Do you want to do what we can now?"

"Yes," he says, rooting around in his pocket for a pencil.

4
Joe

Two seconds before the 6B bell I scan the rows for attendance and possible tremors. Seismography. Three or four kids have actually started to write in their journals already; no one has voiced a complaint—yet; Jerry is not wearing his hat; Mike has a pencil. Allen is in his assigned desk, the front legs of which are tipped back to just one hair before no return. I ignore this. Wait a minute . . . "Where's Joe?" His name was not on the absence list.

"With his wo-man," someone says.

Joe's woman: diaphanous, with a mass of murky hair. Named Summer.

The bell rings and I scribble myself a note to check on this later: *9/20 Joe ???*. But when I look up, there he is in his seat, head bent, already writing, settled in as though he's been here for hours. I look at the class and roll my eyes. Most of them are grinning, no doubt having just witnessed what I missed—Joe's silent sprint from door to desk. They watch to see what will happen next. But Joe just keeps on working. The model student.

We *do* admire his style.

With a minimum of diversionary activity most of the rest of the class start their five minute journals. Steve, Mike, and Jerry aren't writing yet, but they're holding their pencils in the air and squinting. Mind-sweeping or the appearance thereof. I take a handful of raisins from Allen just as he's about to flick the first one across the room and know he'll now refuse to do any work today. Third week of school: Some are wearing down and some aren't.

I move around the room picking up the folders of those absent: Patty and Vance. Must remember to also check again with the office about Vance's continued failure to be present. As I pass behind Joe, I whisper, "Nice timing." He smiles with mock innocence and pushes his journal toward me:

> *shes dresed in red*
> *and lookin fine*
> *tonights the night*
> *Im gona make her mine*

I nod in appreciation and he continues. Joe often writes rhymed love poems, but he will never leave any of them in his file. He always folds them neatly and tucks them in his pocket. No way, he tells us. These are for my woman.

With well-defended students like Allen, it's hard to ever get beyond stand-off, but someone like Joe just can't resist the beat, the pulsing of words. Besides liking to write poems, Joe likes to talk—his opinions on what's what in the world. And to think. He often caught the subtler themes of the movies we watched last year. He liked to speculate: Why Terry Malloy cared so much about his pigeons in *On the Waterfront*, why the camera showed Neal's father's slippers lined up exactly side by side in *Dead Poets Society*. He listens with fixed attention to our oral reading of *Cool World,* sometimes echoing the 50's Harlem dialect that grabs him: "The reason summer time such a gas and a fake is because it come on like it gonna last forever." And Joe's listening comprehension is high. Often he calls out astute answers before I finish the questions. Already this year on his way into class, I've asked him quietly, Today, hold off a little so everyone has a chance to think the questions through for a few seconds.

But Joe will not read. Don't give me a part, he always says. I don't do that oral jazz. And he doesn't do the silent kind either. The past two years we've had short independent reading units. The first big goal: to be able to focus and read for one half hour with the whole room still, nothing but breathing and the turning of pages. They may read anything: hunting magazines, the newspaper, animal picture books, *Seventeen*, transitional novels, little high-interest/low-vocabulary stories—anything, as long as they follow those words across space. Sometimes, three days a week for two or three weeks in a row, that worked.

The second goal was for students who could, to stay with it to actually read a whole book, some of it outside of class. A few did. But the most Joe usually conceded was to be semi-quiet while he flipped through *Rolling Stone* and *Hot Rod* ads. It helped the rest of the class if he took a long trip to the bathroom and back. Cheers have not encouraged him. Neither has hip material: *The Far Side*, sophisticated comics like *Raw*, Jim Morrison lyrics and poems. Neither have independent excursions to the library, the hope that if he bounced around that much print, some title would hit him. None has.

Day after day he turned in his reading record empty. Partly it's because he does not read well, but surely it's more than that. Maybe it just does not interest him to go off alone at such a slow speed. No way.

In the blank beside *Social Development* on Joe's Individualized Education Plan, the resource room teacher has written "very streetwise." But it often seems to me that Joe feels torn between being "good" and the excitement of the edge. And Joe has more options than the rest of the class. He's one of the few kids in 6B who has social mobility. A BOCES student who can cross over to the "in-crowd." His girlfriend moves on the same fringes and takes the college prep courses like chemistry and trig. Joe doesn't play sports, but he hunts and rides dirt bikes with Dale Henderson, the English 12 boy who is so open in his journals and class discussion and one of the most popular boys in the school.

Last year Joe's mother remarried, and soon after, Joe got a haircut and removed his skeleton earring. He started wearing sweatshirts that bore the bold lettering of colleges and teams: Michigan, The Steelers. I received a note from home written in a square even hand: *Please let us know if Joseph is not keeping up with his work. Or if he is impolite.* For several weeks Joe came early to class; he sat up straighter in his desk; he was quiet during silent reading. He even entered the numbers of pages he was looking over and copied a few phrases from ads on his reading record. At times his brow was actually creased with his efforts at reform. Wow, I thought, is this possible? Such a quick transformation? He stopped dancing in and calling out, but he also stopped participating. He no longer helped the class with clarification when I messed up and the group wasn't getting it. He stopped blurting out the answers to the tough questions. He stopped dazzling us with his wit. What's wrong with you, Joe? a couple of the kids around him asked after several days of such stillness. Are you sick or something? someone said. Woman trouble, Neal suggested. But Joe just shrugged and kept on being perfect.

Then one day I noticed he was back in his suede jacket and his black T-shirt with AC/DC emblazoned across his chest. His hair started to get longer and the earring dangled once again. I did write several notes home when his reading record returned to its former blankness, but there was no response. No return phone calls.

One Monday soon after this gradual backslide, Joe popped in right on the bell. He stood in front of the class, brimming with his old joie de vivre. He played air guitar while he sang us a few bars of "Shake Me All Night Long."

Neal thrust a phantom microphone forward and asked, We wonder why you waste your time around here? and Joe jumped in with his standard reply: When I could take it on the road.

Sorry as I was to see the emptiness of his reading record, I admit, along with the rest of the class, it was good to have Joe back.

5
Vance

Eighth period I run through my reminder notes: Vance??? I look over this quarter's attendance so far. Instead of day after day marking the little boxes next to Vance's name *a, a, a,* I write down a *P* whenever he makes a surprise appearance. This is the second year Vance has been enrolled, but seldom present, in Improvement of Language Skills. Already less than a month into the new school year and he has returned to the same pattern: He's been absent all week. My main image of Vance—a blank space.

And Vance's cumulative writing folder is empty as well. I know that two or three times last year he did pass his paper up the row. One of them was half a page on how he liked to ride his bike. A Raleigh Racer. Neat handwriting. The words correctly spelled. But what happened to these papers upon their return is part of the "gone without a trace" pattern of students like Vance. Self-erasing.

I find Marie Baker, the woman in charge of the attendance records, busy spreading out the cards for all the students absent today, a pencil in her teeth, her glasses nested on the top of her gray head. Marie has worked at the school for years, has seen the administrators come and go, the forms required by the state quadruple. She grew up in Stanton, went to this school, married a boy from her class. Her children graduated from Stanton Central. Now their children go here. She knows the histories of most of the students, their parents and grandparents. During the hard times that seem to cycle through school systems, she maintains that steady long view: We will survive.

"Vance," I say to her.

"I know," she says. "I've called his mother every morning this week. Poor woman."

Marie leans her head on her hands and sighs. "His mother says she can't do anything with him and now he's sixteen. She's been telling us that since he was seven. And it's the truth, she can't."

"So has he officially withdrawn?"

"Nothing that definite," she tells me. She sees my frustration. "Everything's been done and then some. For years."

She means that for years social services, the courts, the school have been making visits, making plans, threatening foster-home placement, counseling, but always no matter what, it turns to dust. Vance shows up for a while, but before too long, he's truant. And now he's sixteen.

"Poor woman," she says again. "Poor Vance. I'll call tomorrow morning if he doesn't show up."

I decide I'll give it a shot. Marie writes down Vance's number. I use the phone in the nurse's office just beyond Marie's desk. I'd like to close the door, but I don't. As the phone rings and rings, I try to think how to pitch my entreaty. Just as I'm about to hang up, Vance's groggy voice says, "Yeah."

"Vance, this is . . ." and then there's a dial tone.

When a student's attendance is as sporadic as Vance's for months, for years, it's hard not to finally drop him in the "Hello, Vance, it's good to see you" groove. Whenever he is in school, which was a total of thirty-nine days up until March last year when he disappeared completely, I try to keep giving him the message that it's never too late, that today's the day he could turn it around. The space is there for him to move into if he wants to. I keep clueing him in one-on-one with enough "context" for him to plug into that day's work if he so chooses. On the other hand I stop carrying him around in my mind, let the weight of his more and more back-work pass from me.

Why kids don't want to sit next to Vance, I don't know. Personal hygiene. A social outcast. A certain spookiness. Adolescent cruelty. Teachers do what they can to minimize the drawing away.

Usually Vance is as passive as you can get and still keep moving: dark glasses, dark jacket, monosyllabic. But early last year for a brief period, he was different. He had been in class several days in a row. He wasn't wearing his shades. We were working on building up confidence. Each day the last five minutes of the period, we drew one student's name from a box. This student then had to sit at the podium to be interviewed from a list of questions the class had made up: What's your favorite music group? Can you talk to your parents? How do you feel about abortion? And so forth. A student had the right to "pass" on any question he/she didn't feel like answering, and the class was bound to the rule of being supportive. If your name was called, you absolutely had to be interviewed. We would allow you to stay in your seat and turn toward the class if the podium seemed too risky.

The interviews were going well. We'd been through about half the group. No one had refused. Then Vance's name got pulled. And he was actually in class. There was a moment of silence. I was just about to tell him that he could be interviewed from his seat when he got up and shambled to the front.

The room became completely quiet, that stillness of wonder. Vance was here. Vance was sitting up at the podium. Vance was looking at us. Vance, whose sparse communication up until now had consisted of nods, grunts, and shrugs, was about to speak. Maybe.

I remember Joe went first. A godsend. "What is your favorite rock group?"

"Metalica," Vance said.

I was busy trying to look like there was nothing surprising in all this and hoping all would keep floating along for another three or four minutes.

Stan was next. I held my breath.

"What is your favorite hobby?" Stan asked, without a trace of irony.

"Bike riding," Vance told him.

One by one—Neal, Rich, even Jerry—asked easy, friendly questions: the kind of car he'd like—a Mustang; his favorite food—fried chicken. So far so good. We covered about seven more questions, with Vance answering each one briefly, but without hesitation, and looking out at us the whole time.

About half a minute before the bell, I thanked him and he sat down, smiling.

Wow!

After class I went down to talk to Will Booker about how well Vance had done, that we needed to be alert to helping him build on this new energy. Will Booker runs the "time out" center, a place for kids to go and talk it over, to cool down, the in-school suspension area, a kind of hodgepodge of needs, and he's really good at it, with lots of contact with kids' parents. We were both optimistic, ready to reinforce Vance the next day.

But Vance wasn't in class the next day, or the next. Calls were made home. I mailed some work to him with an encouraging note. Will Booker met with Vance and his mother. Agreements were made. The rest of the week, no sign of Vance. Several times he'd come in on the school bus, but then had disappeared and hadn't been on the BOCES run.

Will and I talked to Joe Marsh, the guidance counselor. We talked to the school psychologist. I said sometimes I felt like Vance was the kind of kid who might one day open fire on a playground or his mother. That kind of quiet, I said. They nodded their heads in agreement. More calls and referrals were made. Time sucked away at anything definite.

Weeks later I looked up one day to see Vance wandering into 6B, dark glasses and jacket. Holed up again. Hello, Vance, I said. It's good to see you.

Marie turns to me and shrugs when I start to put down the phone, but then I stop and dial the number again and let it ring and ring some more. The Vance who shambled up to the podium, who looked out at us and answered every question loud and clear has got to be someplace in that house.

6
Allen

Allen, please don't squeak your sneakers back and forth on the floor.

Allen, don't throw staples. Please put the stapler back on the table.

Allen, when the fire whistle goes off, please do not get up and go to the window. You need to sit down and complete the five-minute journal.

Allen, may I please have all of the raisins in your left hand.

Allen, would you step into the hall for a minute so we can talk?
Why did I ask you to come out here to talk to me?

By the third day of classes, I had started to document Allen's behavior. Each day, on a sheet in the back of my plan book, I jotted down what had happened 6B: *9/13 Allen did not do the assigned journal or the reading questions. He refused to resume his seat (vacated to go watch the fire trucks).* One to one in the hall when asked to take responsibility for his actions, he would not make eye contact and stated he wasn't "doing nothing." I told him, if he would cooperate, he would be successful, that I could help him with his work, but that continued disruption would result in his removal.

I checked Allen's test results again. They indicated that he could read on an eighth grade level, the second highest score in the class next to Vic Gantz, with 12 G.L. printed after his name.

I met with Joe Marsh during my planning period.

"Allen's got one toe over the line a lot of the time," I said. "I'm keeping a record. If his disruption continues, I want to have him removed from the class."

"He signed the contract," Joe said. "He's cooperative or he will be placed in a more structured situation: the resource room or back in self-contained at BOCES."

I ignored the behaviors that did not interrupt what we were doing. The class watched to see how it went with Allen. It was important for all of us that he get straight soon.

In a relatively small rural school (700 students K-12), teachers often end up teaching all of the children in a family. I taught some of Allen's older siblings: his brother, Cliff Lange, about sixteen years earlier, a pale thin boy, in trouble with the local authorities at a young age, and Connie, a bold, bright sister. I first knew Connie when I did some writing workshops with her fourth grade class. She wrote a wonderful story about a girl and her horse. Later when Connie got to high school, she was already on an in-and-out school pattern, quitting and returning and quitting again. Sometimes as part of probation requirements. When she did turn up in a class, she was quick to declare her territory. She wasn't really looking for trouble, but know this: She wasn't taking any shit from nobody, the teacher included. She wore leather and hip-hugger jeans, with a slice of flesh showing. I liked her and respected her clarity. Finally after a few years of this go-for-a-month, out-for-two routine, almost sixteen and still in ninth grade, Connie was just gone and I didn't see her again.

I remember when Allen was born. When Cliff was in eighth grade. At the local grocery I saw their tired mother, an older woman who also kept foster children, with a shrieking red-headed child stuck in a cart that was mounded and threatening to spill over. Allen. I remember smiling at her and the flailing child, sending her sympathetic vibes and feeling very grateful.

A few days after Allen and I had gotten nowhere in the hall, Allen entered subdued.

"I need all my work for the next week," he said.

"What's up?" I asked.

He told me his family was going to Florida. I expressed my concern about his being out so soon in the school year, that I felt this was an important time for him to get settled in.

"We'll be back in a week or two," he said.

During my planning period, I assembled the *Cool World* chapters* we'd probably cover in the next ten days, along with the quizzes and a list of suggested journal topics. At the end of the day I took the folder down to him in the resource room, where he spent the rest of the afternoon after his mornings in Automotive Technology at BOCES and his 6B ILS class.

"It's important that you get this done so you'll know what's going on when you get back," I told him as I leafed through the work to show him what he needed to do.

"There's a lot of it," he said.

Several weeks later when Allen returned, after asking about his trip, I asked him how he did with the *Cool World* reading and the journals.

"I lost the folder," he said.

"How far did you get on the reading?" I asked.

"Not too far," he told me.

I handed him the chapters we'd be doing that day and asked various people in the class to summarize what he'd missed. They told him: Duke, the 14 year old main character, the one telling the story, is trying to buy this piece, that's a gun, from Priest, who's not a priest, but really is a fence, that's someone who sells stolen stuff, but Duke is having a lot of trouble raising the fifteen dollars, which was a lot of money in Harlem back in the 1950s. And Duke wants the gun because his gang—the Royal Crocodiles—are getting ready to go down on the Wolves, which means have a rumble. He says he needs the gun to be cool, but we know it's really because he's scared.

My impression was that Allen wasn't hearing much of this.

We began to do the next chapter out loud as a play, "the big night an how it all happen." Since Vic refused all long parts, and he was the only one in the class who could have handled the long sections of 50's Harlem dialect, I did the first person narration, but Kathy, Cindy, Joan, Mike, Patty, and Lori were willing to be the various gang members when they had dialogue: Duke, Blood, Rod, Cowboy, Lu

Ann, and Cherokee. Most of the class was involved in the book; we were gathering momentum. This was one of the best scenes: a knife fight between Rod and Cowboy in the Crocodile "club house," a tenement apartment, with no lights or heat.

I saw that Allen was not with us. I touched his desk which he had tipped way back. He lowered it. We started to read, with me standing close to Allen, hoping to keep him on track.

> Rod eyes they all narrow you know an he study Cowboy.
> "None of that now." I tell them. But they don't hear me. When a mans blood rise he don't hear nothin but the blood an he dont see nothin but the man in front who soundin him.
> Rod say. "You soundin me Cowboy?
> Cowboy give him that big smile whut aint a smile.

At this point Lori lost her place for Duke's dialogue so I moved away from Allen's desk to point to the line. A half minute later when I turned back, Allen was just slipping a large chartreuse squirt gun back into his jacket and Calvin was wiping his face.

I stepped to the phone, dialed, and loud enough for them all to hear, I said, "Mr. Marsh, Allen's on his way. Perhaps he'll tell you all about it."

I opened the door, motioned Allen out, and closed it behind him. "Fourth paragraph, page 74. Lori, it's your part."

> "Break it up," I warn them. An the guys putten down they glasses of muscatel an slow movin out of the way. I jus sit there with my muscatel an watch Cowboy an Rod both. Especially Rod cause it up to him to make the move.

10/2 Allen Lange permanently removed from 6B class.

*Since *Cool World* by Warren Miller has long been out of print it has been a tricky thing to go on teaching it. More than a decade ago the original set of paperbacks, after being glued and retaped many times, had to be discarded. The pages actually started to crumble. Even my teacher copy mysteriously disappeared, so that for many years I was without the book and I felt it as a loss. Then one day in the dusky far-reaches of a secondhand book store on 14th Street, voila!

Soon after the initiation of the ILS program, obtaining a class set of *Cool World* became important: to help poor readers come to know the magic words can do; how finally there are truths that only fiction can let us feel. Even in a more homogeneous group like ILS, the range of language ability is wide, so the difficult thing is how to sometimes find rich printed material that everyone will have access to in terms of decoding as well as emotional appeal. The problem, of course, of high interest-low vocabulary books is that they seldom make you want to get up and dance. And unless you're dancing and singing, there are certain truths you cannot feel: Hello, sorrow and joy; here you are again. Welcome. Though certainly books like S.E. Hinton's *The Outsiders* have reached many students on both levels: easy to read and emotionally engaging. According to the *World Almanac*, even 30 years after it was written, *The Outsiders* is still the book most high school students name as their favorite. (And sadly it is the only book that many high school kids have ever word-for-word read.) Still, for me as a teacher the language and characterization in *The Outsiders* became pretty thin by the third year of re-reading. Of course I can continue to use it with a class and it can go well, but I cannot fake that electricity, and that is inevitably a lessening of the energy of the unit.

Finding dynamite reading material like *Cool World* remains a problem when working with poor readers, especially when a good title goes out of print. However, my experience in teaching has almost always been that if you really want to do something with a class, there is a way to work it out. Since no books were to be had, and since *Cool World* is a short novel of less than 200 pages, photocopying and collating it one chapter at a time became "the way." (Can I with impunity confess to breaking the copyright laws here in print?)

As part of this process the print could be enlarged 100 percent and still fit on the standard page, a BIG help to some problem readers. Also, it worked well to pass out just the chapters we'd be able to cover in a period, with students automatically sending the sections just read to the back table to be returned to the individual chapter folders by an organized, willing student like Kathy. I wanted to use these same photocopies again and again with other classes. Clearly making twenty copies of a 200 page book was not something I could often do. Conquering a book a few chapters at a time was less overwhelming; every day we really got somewhere. Plus each chapter was often a little vignette with wonderful titles like "the time the old lady got eat by the dog," "We go down," "After the big night," so this presentation highlighted the structure.

Though I've used *Cool World* many times with students, it still lives for me. I want to read it with them in the same way I want to roller-skate to organ music and dance to Dylan. Books with this kind of rhythm of language and power of image we often read aloud—no matter how well the students could manage the material alone. If many people in the class read well, we usually alternate with me or one of the best readers just reading the chapter to us while we follow along, and then doing the next chapter as a play. I assign only a chapter or two for nightly homework, with no homework on the nights the next part is too good to be done silently since so many of today's students (even the better ones) do not make vivid movies in their minds.

Obviously when doing so much of a book out loud—probably one third as play, one third single oral reader, and one third for homework—the teacher has to keep the class moving. Units of more than five weeks or so are hard to sustain no matter how great the material. And of course with a group like ILS, all the reading must be done in class. No homework. Certainly all students are encouraged to fly on to read the book at home on their own in a few days if they can, and then to be willing to poke along with us in class a second time to hear the music and more fully see how the images pile up to make the world. In English 10 and English 12 a few do just that. In ILS Joan and Lori and Kathy will occasionally go on ahead.

Often the books that beg to be done orally have strong first person voices: *To Kill A Mockingbird* by Lee, *This Boy's Life* by Wolff, *Great*

Expectations by Dickens, *The Things They Carried* by O'Brien, and some stories by Richard Wright, T.C.Boyle, Poe, Frank O'Connor, Welty, Flannery O'Connor, Dylan Thomas, Capote, Dahl, and Salinger. These are a few of the titles and authors that are the current favorites which leap into my mind.

Most students can in one or two periods, with me ready to cue quietly, learn how to read the chapter as a play, adjusting to the leaving off of the tags like "Jem said," and the recognition of their dialogue part even if it has no tag. Usually there are four or five students in ILS who are willing to leap in, and that's usually plenty for a scene. On the board before the period begins I often list the students' names next to the character they'll play that period. That way I can keep rotating the parts and we never have to break the rhythm of the action to look for someone to be Little Chuck Little right in the middle of the cootie scene in *Mockingbird*.

Beyond delivering any one literary work more completely to a student, this continual hearing of literature helps students to become better silent readers (and writers), for slowly they learn to internalize these rhythms, to more accurately register the writer's tone, to image the particulars that slowly bring the characters forward as complex beings—to say nothing of beginning to notice these telling details in the creatures who people their own world. The beginning steps to seeing they are not "other," to recognizing our common humanity. And grace.

About ten years ago I took a wonderful course on D.H. Lawrence. I was there on a waiver for working with a student teacher, my first literature course in twenty years. I had forgotten how exciting it was to be a student in a challenging class. For me the adventure of this course was part of a general reawakening to the wonder of language, and a good testimonial to the need for teachers to continue taking courses and meeting in workshops with other lovers of words. At the end of the term as the professor looked out over the small, scattered group of nine graduate students and myself, he said, Nothing personal, but I like Lawrence so much that even if none of you were here, I'd look forward to coming into these rooms to read his work.

Teachers need to have that kind of passion as a wellspring, but the day that Tom Robinson goes up to be questioned by Atticus, when

Tobias Wolff tells us how he cannot apologize to the Welsh's for stealing their gas, when O'Brien helps us see the face of the dead Vietnamese soldier, when Duke tells us how he calls and calls for LuAnn, all these need to be heard out loud and sitting together. It's important that we witness these words.

Winter

7
How To

6B starts to seep in. First, the ones who knock themselves out trying to get it right, hoping maybe this will keep them safe "out there"— Kathy and Calvin. Me. Kathy gets the little player and tapes of *The Kitchen God's Wife* out of my drawer, thinking we may have reading the second part of the period. Calvin orders his papers and folds his hands on the desk, ready. A few more wander in: Cindy, Rich, Neal. Neal sits down on my stool at the podium and pretends to be studying the Daily Attendance list, the one that every day says at the top *Learning to Care; Caring to Learn*. I shake my head "no" at him. He pretends he doesn't see me. I start to move toward him. Just before I penetrate his space, he slides into his seat and slouches down. He and Rich start to laugh. Joe jives in. The last thing Joe wants is to be sitting in a desk for the next 42 minutes.

I try to be ready for all of them. Ready for every glitch that can push the class into chaos. I know better, but I can't stop doing it. Everything the class will need this period is on their desks and I've centered my mind. I stand at the door as-if-ing total calm. I welcome Patty, who's been out for four days. I tell her if she wants to make up any of the work, she should see me. She tells me she's probably quitting anyway. As usual Vic and Jerry hang outside in the hall until just after the last possible second. As I'm about to close the door, they push themselves in.

"What's this?" Jerry says.

I see I've accidentally put the wrong book on his desk, a copy of *Where the Red Fern Grows*. "That's Joan's. Please put it on the table."

Just then Joan comes in.

Jerry sweeps the book onto the floor and holds his nose, "I'm not touching her book."

"Fuck you," Joan tells him.

I retrieve the book and hand it to her.

"That's enough, Jerry," I say.

Joan sits down and the room gets mostly quiet. I breathe and take in the back rows, the November gray of the hills across the valley. "All right, let's get started," I tell them. Mentally I notice who's not there. Just Vance and Lori. This tallies with the attendance list which is good because my phone has been out for a month so if someone is absent who shouldn't be, it gets complicated to communicate this with the office. Another delay in getting started.

I introduce the new composition unit: process writing. I've already placed on each desk before the class arrives a packet of five pieces of composition paper with a bright yellow sheet stapled on top stating the objectives:

> __ *To be able to write clear step-by-step directions.*
> __ *To be able to catch your own mistakes by carefully proofreading out loud to your partner.*

I pick yellow like the suns they drew in kindergarten, back when maybe they believed. I'm hoping this writing unit will draw on their talents, areas they feel confident in. You know, I tell them, things like How to Drive a Tractor, How to Make a Cake.

"How to . . ." Neal moves his fist rapidly up and down under his desk. Jerry and Rich laugh.

I tell them we'll be using the same basic routine we used for the True Story journals: The first three days of the week, the first ten minutes of each period, they'll be listing the "how to" steps in complete sentences, Thursdays they'll organize one of their lists into a rough draft paragraph or two, and after they've carefully checked these alone and with a partner and I've done any corrections missed, they'll do their final copies on Fridays. Maybe half of them are listening.

"I'm sick of writing," someone says.

Vance comes in. He's wearing his coat. He's always wearing his coat, his navy jacket, zipped to the neck. He hasn't been in class for a couple of weeks. What urge moves him to drop by from time to time? I ask him if he has a pass. He shakes his head no. I ask him if the office knows he's in school. He nods. I fish his folder out of the box and hand it to him.

"All right, I want everyone to list five things you know how to do."

"I can't think of anything," Patty says.

Stan gets out of his seat and takes the bathroom pass off the clipboard.

"Stan, could you wait a few minutes until you understand what we're doing?"

"I have to go," he says, gesturing toward his crotch.

"Sign out," I tell him.

"Since when?"

"Since yesterday." He was absent when I explained that I would prefer that everyone go to the bathroom before they come to class, but if they must leave, they are to sign out and in. They know this is because Joe and Jerry and Stan go every day, each one staying out a *long* time.

Stan signs out and lets the door slam behind him.

"All right, list five things you know how to do." I read them five of mine I've already written on the board: build a fire, make bread, shampoo carpet . . . I tell them not all topics have to be dead serious. "You could do something like How to . . ."

"Skip school," Vance says.

"Or how to pick your nose," Mike adds.

"There's not enough to that, not enough steps."

"Oh, I don't know," Jerry says, "First you put your finger in; then you poke it around until you get a good one . . ."

"Then pull it out and eat it," someone whispers.

"That's gross. You're disgusting," Cindy hollers to the whole group of boys.

"All right," I say, "whatever, but make some of them things that have a real process. The idea is to do the thing in your mind and then try to explain each step clearly to someone who's never done it. Like you're writing a manual."

"A sex manual," Neal says.

Stan has returned, banging the door again and now he's bouncing around the front of the room looking for trouble.

"Sit down," I tell him. "All right now everyone should have five things."

"I can't think of anything."

"This is stupid."

"I've got seven."

"Stan, either sit or you'll have to go down to Mr. Booker's and have a lunch detention."

He continues to wander, picking up my pen, the attendance sheets. He pokes Rich. "Not me. I'm not coming in for lunch."

I write him a pass to go to Mr. Booker's. On the back I write, *DISRUPTIVE*. He leaves. I am supposed to call Mr. Booker to let him know a student's on his way, but with my phone out, this isn't possible. I make a mental note to check later to see if he got there.

"Lighten up," Joe says. "He didn't do anything."

My neck is aching.

"All right, now I want to go around the room and have everyone tell one thing they know how to do. I'll write them on the board. If you see any you can use, write them on your list. You start, Calvin."

"Mow the lawn."

I write that on the board. Meanwhile Joe has turned around so that he is sitting backwards at his desk. He is trying to engage Vic in arm wrestling.

"Are you going or staying?" I ask him.

"Let me think about it," he says.

I continue around the room, writing down one for each of the students: track deer, clean a gun, bow hunt, change the oil in the car, do the laundry. I notice only Calvin and Kathy are copying any.

"Change a baby," Joan says. She has a one year old daughter. Joan is fifteen.

"Now I want to have us do one together on the board that you can copy as we go."

"That's dumb," someone says.

"That way you'll understand how to do your own lists. Let's do How to Change a Tire. How many of you know how to change a tire?" Not one of them raises a hand.

Joe is still fooling around so I write out a pass for him to go to the office. "Come on," I say, "I'm sure some of you know how to change a tire." Poker faces stare back at me. I hand Joe the pass. He swings his suede jacket over his shoulder and moseys out. I follow him into the hall, keeping the door ajar just enough so that the class knows I'm listening. "I'll talk to you later," I tell him.

"Right," he says. He whistles as he goes down the stairs. It's likely he will stop in the 2nd floor bathroom to comb his hair. Recently I asked Joe why he did not go to the 3rd floor bathroom. It would save time. Because it doesn't have a mirror, he said.

I've already worked it out with the school secretary that if any of my 6B class arrive, she's just to hold them there until the next period. She knows I'll be down to check on if, when, and what later.

I write the heading on the board and the words *How to Change a Tire* and under that *Steps:*. I advise them to copy this on the first sheet of composition paper. Mike, Rich, and Vic make no move to write. I tap Mike's desk, catch Vic's eye, whisper, "Get going" to Rich.

"I haven't got a pencil," Mike tells me.

I hand him one from the bunch I have ready. In this class an idle hand is indeed a devil's workshop.

"Now this is not something I really know how to do so you'll be the experts."

Cindy moves closer to the board.

"Okay what do we do first?"

"Loosen the lugs," Cindy says.

"No," Jerry says, "first you better tell them to get the jack and spare out of the trunk."

I see that every single kid in the class is engaged, even Vic, from an ironic distance. One of those magical moments. I cross my fingers. Let it last.

"Good," I say, "Let's take Jerry's first and Cindy's as the second step. Now copy this exactly. Full sentences. Skip lines so we have room to fix it." I start writing on the board. *1. Remove* then I cross that out and write *Get...*

"Make up your mind."

"That's the way it is," I tell them. "When you write, you have to keep changing things."

I continue printing: *Get the jack...* Do we need to mention the other part?"

"What other part?" Vic says.

"The piece you stick in the jack to make it go up and down? Maybe we should include that in parenthesis."

"Every idiot knows you call it a lug wrench," Jerry says.

"I didn't," I tell them.

They all laugh.

"Remember these are instructions for someone who doesn't know much."

"Maybe you better tell them how to open up the trunk in that case."

"No, we'll assume they've got basic common sense."

By now I've got the first step on the board.

"Now, Cindy, the second step."

Slowly we proceed. Vic, Cindy, Rich, and Jerry really know. Their bodies are on Alert. They are discussing it between themselves. Everyone else is listening and diligently copying. I am the secretary. I write and cross out as they negotiate the language. Sometimes I ask questions. "Yeah, but what happens when you can't get the lug nuts off? That happened to me once. When I couldn't get them off, after struggling for an hour, screaming and near tears, I walked a few miles in the freezing cold to a friend's house. She drove me back and you know what she did?"

"She jumped on the wrench," Cindy says.

"That's right." Cindy is beaming. I go back and write, (*If the lug nuts won't turn, you can try jumping . . .*"

"If you keep adding stuff, we're never going to finish," Mike says. I glance at his paper. He is only a few numbers behind the rest of the class. This is perhaps the longest he's stayed with any writing task so far. I look at the rest of them. We've been at this for twenty totally focused minutes. I see by a few bodies, time is about to run out. I cheer them on with, "Hang on. We're almost done. Okay, we've got the spare on and the car back down on the ground. Now what do we do?" I write *10*.

"Tighten the nuts hard," Vic says.

"Not too tight, you'll strip them," Jerry interrupts. "Just get them snug."

I write the instruction. I go back and add "ly" to snug. "Snugly."

"That sounds stupid," Jerry says.

"Yeah, it does," I agree. Tighten snug. Tighten snugly. I'm trying figure which way is best. I erase the "ly"; then I add it back on. "I can't think which way feels right," I tell them.

"You don't know? You're the teacher, and you don't know?" several say with indignation.

I debate whether I want to get anywhere near a discussion of adverbs. I decide I do not. Again I erase the "ly."

"Will you make up your mind," Mike moans.

"Well, let's go with 'snug' because, like Jerry says, it sounds better."

They gaze at me puzzled, like what's the big deal, snug, snugly?

I stand back from the board and skim what we have so far. "But why can't you tighten them all the way when the car's jacked up?"

Jerry looks at me with sympathy. "Same reason you started to loosen them with the car on the ground. The road gives you . . ."

"Resistance," Vic says.

"Yeah."

The tire is on; the car is down.

"Maybe you better tell them to put the stuff back in the trunk," Joan says.

"No," Kathy tells her, "that's just common sense."

"Maybe you should remind them to get their tire fixed so they'll have a spare," Patty says.

"No, no more, enough already," they call out.

The spell is broken. The room starts to wiggle.

"All right, pass in your sheets. You did really well with that. Now tomorrow you'll pick your own topic and do the same thing." Most of them are not listening. The lunch bell is in one minute. Neal and Rich and Mike try to go up to put their folders away early. I push them back with my eyes, my hands extended in a Stop Right There signal. I collect the papers.

Most of them lean out of their seats like runners crouched for the gun.

The bell rings and they are off.

8
Neal

My mailbox is jammed with junk. Mostly fund-raiser packets for class advisors and brochures from publishers and travel bureaus. Would I like to take a group of students to Europe over spring break? For a moment I imagine a tour with 6B. Oh my! Sandwiched between a candy sale leaflet and a copy of the faculty meeting minutes is a note from Mr. Booker: *Please send down work for Neal Thomas. He'll be on in-school suspension all afternoon.* I wonder what Neal did to be removed from a half-day of classes, but I'm not surprised. He's been cruising the edge the last couple of weeks.

I have mixed feelings about in-school suspension. So often it's used with "acting-out" students who are already behind in their work, who feel no great loss about being denied the privilege of attending class for a day or two. If the student is sent to an area where the atmosphere is penal, where the person supervising is authoritarian, where you're simply isolated for a day, then often I think it's just more easy fuel for a student who's already burning. Still, the way Will Booker structures the situation offers the possibility for getting back on track for some students. After the suspendee has a quiet time of looking at the three walls of a study carrel, Will makes himself available for counsel and help with assignments. He's a good listener and the students know he cares. He can sometimes defuse and mediate. And I must admit respite from Neal's energy is welcome today. He has been so lewd lately it will be pleasant to have a break from his double entendres.

I write out his assignment and stick it in Mr. Booker's box along with Neal's folder. I don't feel too optimistic that Neal will do the writing and revising work. Neal hates to write. He is one of the few 6B students who likes to read, but his writing performance is dutiful at best. He writes the minimum and never from the heart. He mumbles and swears as he moves down the page as though he grudges every word. And he purposely chooses a topic that in no way will interest himself or the reader. The subtext is always the same: This is so stupid. You can make me write, but you can't make me say anything that matters.

Fifth period, after the BOCES bus arrives and I know Neal will be settled into a carrel, I go down to the "time-out" room to make sure Neal understands the assignment. It's an all-purpose basement room, low-ceilinged and carpeted, but without a single window. Once it was the school "dungeon" where boxes of records, broken furniture, stacks of outdated textbooks were stashed, but like most schools Stanton is short on space so it was converted. Though it still gives off that "down under" feel, the room is big and really ideal for having five things going on at once. In addition to this being Will Booker's area, the room is also headquarters for the Liberty Partnership worker, a grant program to give support for all kinds of student activities, and the "office" of the Community-School liaison person, both of whom are presently coordinating a trip to New York in their little partitioned section. There are carrels around two sides of the room and four or five students are working at these or at least sitting quietly, staring. Will is at his desk over in one far corner meeting with a student and her parents—the mother, anxious; the father, angry. Several students are working at computers, putting together a monthly newspaper, and one of the honor society seniors is tutoring some middle school kids at a big table in the center with two cheerleaders making posters on the opposite end. And the room is quiet—a real testament to how good Will Booker is at this.

Neal is at a far carrel; he's reading. I peer over his shoulder: *The Outsiders.*

"How many times does this make?" I ask him.

"Nine," he tells me, without looking up and with the appearance that he's still reading.

Though I already know the answer, I ask him anyway. "Do you want me to go over the class assignment with you?"

He shakes his head no and turns the page.

Will Booker gives me a sign with both of his hands pushing down through the air—all will be as it is. He will get to Neal when the time is right.

Just then Rich and Stan peek in from the hall, trying to get Neal's attention. Mr. Booker looks at them and points his finger definitively: Get where you are supposed to be. Now. They disappear.

I follow behind them as they double-step it up to the library. Just as they make the turn, Stan yells back, "You should see what Neal drew on the wall in the library yesterday."

I stop by Emma Lowe's office at the end of the library. She is changing a DVD while she anxiously watches the BOCES returnees through the door.

"What did Neal draw on the wall? I'm assuming that's why he's on in-school suspension."

Her lips tighten and she looks pained, "I can't even say it," she says, "but I demanded that the custodians paint over it. I said I wasn't going to open up the library until that…that filth was gone. They came in early this morning and did that whole section."

I pass through into the library and the smell of paint. Rich, Stan, and Joe are inspecting the yellow area behind the dictionary stand.

"Too bad you missed it, Mrs. H.," Joe says. "Neal's Masterpiece. I predict our boy Neal has a real future as a porn artist."

The first time I saw Neal he was in fifth grade. Freckled, with eyes snapping behind the big round frames of his glasses. The kind of kid it's hard not to reach out to run your hand down over his cowlick, to squeeze his skinny little-boy neck. He appeared in my room one day. Could he and another kid have my door to do for the Christmas door decorating contest? I remember their earnest efforts for days. The careful taping of the red construction paper background, the sleigh, the reindeer. And finally the gluing on of dozens of small cotton ball dots of snow. Watching them work away so independently and with such purpose filled me with that all's-right-with-the-world spirit. My prediction would have been that Neal had a great future as a sweet person who always remembered his mother's birthday.

Neal is one of seven children, all of whom have been in my English classes. He's the "baby" of the family. The mother always impressed me as a strong woman who had a grip on things: definite times when she expected them to be home with set chores to do around the big, old house they rent out in the country. The children have several different last names. And from time to time there was mention of the comings and goings of fathers.

Neal has read each of the S.E. Hinton books many times. But he is artful in his resistance to writing. Often when we're working on writing, I'll see that he's reading a book in his lap, his jean jacket forming a tent, just the top of his shaved head moving back and forth slightly. He repeated seventh and eighth grade English because he refused to do any of the composition work. I remember Neal's oldest brother, Junior, carving the words, I hate righting, so deeply into the first page of his spiral journal that the next five or six pages repeated the legend. But several of Neal's brothers and sisters were poets. And all seven pulse with energy. A kind of beating of wings longing for flight.

The end of the day Mr. Booker placed Neal's folder back in my box with a note that he had completed his rough draft and final copy as directed and in a spirit of cooperation. Surprised, I opened his folder to read:

Neal Thomas *Free Writing—Final Draft*
ILS 6B *November 27*

I walked out on the porch with mom. She told me to sit my ass down. I did.

"Well, what happened? Joan called me and told me you were sitting in the principal's office. Now what the hell did you do?"

"I got caught smoking up to the football game Friday night. I didn't realize Rotary Park belonged to the school. Mr. Larken came over and started bitching at me for smoking on school property."

"Is that all? Is that the truth? You only got caught smoking on school property?"

"Yes. I did not call Larken names or spit on him. Only smoking."

"Well, I imagine you got in trouble in school. I can't

think of any reason to punish you again."
"All right."
"Next time, give me a reason to punish you. Hit him or call him a bald bastard or something you can get into trouble for."

Burning. Burning with words. But at last writing with a voice, writing that's real.

9
Cindy

Cindy is waving her hand. Her dayglow pink pen stabs the air. I zap her with Be Reasonable vibes: I'll get to you soon. Her hand stays up. Accelerates.

The room is pulsing with uneasiness. It's supposed to be silent reading time, but half the class isn't into it: Joe is drumming his fingers, tapping his toes, his suede jacket already over his shoulder, waiting for the bathroom pass. Jerry has his head down under his baseball hat, pretending to be sleeping. Soft snores. Neal and Rich are playing jab and kick. And Stan has that break-it-down look. Fortunately the TV and VCR are not in the room or without my seeing anything, like Roald Dahl's fingersmith, Stan would have every hookup replugged into the wrong holes; the tracking, horizontal, and color so screwed up, it would take Emma Lowe, our librarian and visual aid person, half a period to de-sabotage the system. All the while shaking her head at me, saying, They'll do this if they get a chance; you have to keep your eye on them. Me, filled with shame, mumbling apologies.

I'm patrolling the room just trying to maintain a demilitarized zone so that Calvin, Joan, Lori, Robert, and Vic can continue to read. I'm the searchlight; they're timing my sweep in order to know when to break for the wall. At least Mike is absent. Thank you.

Softly I'm reading out loud to Stan the beginning of his article on feeding growth hormones to cows and my neck is aching and there are three feet of icy snow outside and more coming and Cindy's jabbing her hand angrily into space and I say in a stage whisper, "Cindy, just go on with what you can do. I'll get to you as soon as I can." Voice full of all of the above.

She glares at me, her lips move, but fortunately, I am far enough away that I can pretend not to hear her response. She sits undecided for a minute, eyeing the door, then she rips a hunk of paper out of her spiral and begins to write furiously.

Maybe Stan is started. I leave him and go quietly up to Cindy's desk, even though I am pretty sure of her response.

"What's your question?" I say in a conciliatory tone.

"Too late now," she hisses, not looking up, and goes on writing.

"Give me a break," I say to her.

Again she eyes the door and then returns to writing.

The class now gets semi-still. As though the energy between Cindy and me sucked up all the loose electricity in the room. As Cindy leaves for her next class, she slaps several pieces of moist paper, still hot with her fluorescent scrawl, into my waiting hand.

I read Cindy's journal after school:

> *Journal 23*
> *November 27*
>
> *If you want to yell and bitch at me why don't bitch at other people in this room. For one Stan is always talking you don't sent him out. just because he needs a lot of help you don't have take it out on me. right now he stand out talking loud to Joan talking loud.*
>
> *Then Joe get up when he want comes in late. he only spend about 20 min in class the tops. He go to the bathroom least 3 time or does something all the guys go and spend least 10 mins going to the bathroom. Plus your sapose to make him cover his marywana shirt How you the I feel about that now if I only spend 20 min of your class out of 45 min. I guess your to busy treails your pet so good. you don't have time to see what the other people want or need or who is hear now Vic has been gone for about 5 min If Joe leave will wrigth it down on the top of this sheet of paper. Jerry just left for the bathroom at 12:30 Joe just go to smoke a cig He even take a cig out of his pocket Vanc just walk in 12:30 first time today with out a pass you didn't even see him at all. Because you all your time w/ Stan you been over there 15 min right now. Next I'm going to clock you how long your with your pet. Now you just notice Vanc was here. Well*

> *Joe is done with his cig 12:35 and Jerry not back yet. Now Stan is walking around talking Patty and Joan. Now Joe and stan are are talking you come and say shhh and that it and there is talking now 12:41 and Jerry stilln't back and been 13 min Jerry just come back 12:46 at is 16 min. Stan start talking you spend 10 min again with him Joe put his folder away Now stan is putting his folder up. I think Joan going write the work over for him.*

The dots on the letter *i* have stabbed through the paper. Ouch! You don't have time to see what other people want or need. After a few minutes of self-defense: What the hell am I supposed to do? . . . I'd like to see how long you'd keep your sanity, I must admit she's close to the mark. It's not fair to let a few students manipulate the situation at the expense of others who need help. I have got to find more effective ways of dealing with Stan, et al. After I get through that punch to the gut, I am struck by a number of things. First of all, half of the behaviors and comings and goings, I missed.

I re-read Cindy's journal. Look how much she has written and how she clearly considers writing a powerful means of communicating and releasing her feelings. But, also look how certain problems we've worked on still persist. Of course this was written in the heat of battle and not proofread at all, but still there are more omissions, more sentences that don't make sense than is usual in journals, even those of the poorest writers. Omissions and not putting stops at the ends of her sentences are the writing problems Cindy and I have been working on most the last couple of years. But "end-stopping" and making sentences clear requires a lot of one-on-one reading out loud, and Cindy's right, I don't get to her often enough and there's no one in 6B who's quite up to such heavy-duty editing.

Cindy and I have had similar skirmishes. This is Cindy's third year in ILS. Once or twice a year she and I have a fight—her bad day matches up with one of mine and we go at it. Both of us have become better at minimizing the damage. Our first year after a heated exchange of a few sentences, I kicked her out and sent her to the office. I even filled out a disciplinary form so that she had to see the principal: "Cindy was uncooperative. She called me a bitch and I told her to go to the office." She vented big time and he got the picture and called me and asked what I had in mind and I said (by then returned to calm), I'd talk with her. Then we apologized to each other.

Her second year we set it up that when the two of us were about to get into it, she could storm out to go down to the Home Ec room to cool off. We have a wonderful Technology (Home Ec) teacher who has really connected with Cindy. She helped negotiate this strategy.

Now we're down to a poison pen letter from her and a return letter from me:

> *Dear Cindy,*
> *Sorry. I was having a bad day.*
> *You're doing well at bringing out your feelings in writing. You're right: the "bathroom going" is getting out of hand (again). I am going to have to deal with it. However, remember we do have our good days in here too. You and many people in the class are making progress in reading, writing, and speaking. Most of the time, I feel like you are pretty understanding and tolerant. I appreciate it when you are willing to help the other students and are able to keep yourself going. I'll try to do better at getting to you when I can see you're frustrated.*
> *Peace,*
Mrs. H.

Like so many students in the class, Cindy has had a hard time. Her mother died when she was little. She's the youngest in a large family that is always boiling over: fights, jail, unwanted pregnancies, alcohol and drug problems, unemployment. When she was sixteen, she moved in with her boyfriend's family where she and her boyfriend were allowed to share a room. He was a year younger. She received no financial aid from her family though she was eligible for some benefits. She chose to buy a car, and in order to make the car payments and buy clothes, she worked thirty hours a week at the Victory Market. And often on my way to school each morning I would see her out helping her boyfriend with his paper route.

Most of Cindy's journals, folders, and notebook covers contain doodles of her boyfriend's name, her first name and his last name. He is the center of many of her writings and conversations. She told me she hated to see him go to college because he might meet someone else. Someone skinny. When he went away on an overnight field trip, she said she couldn't sleep. She said she eats when she's worried. Mostly I just listen and when I can, mention how important it is in a relationship for both people to have lives of their own, but that for many of us this is a hard lesson to learn and even when learned is still a process of rebalancing.

When I pass back the work turned in the day before, Cindy carefully reads my letter. She attaches my response to her journal. Then she goes over to the bookcase. As she hefts the dictionary back to her desk, I notice she's wearing baggy shirts again to cover her weight gain. For a long time I see her turning the pages of the dictionary; then finally she smiles and raises her hand. I move back to her seat. Everyone is pretty settled in today.

"How do you pronounce this word here," she says pointing to the dark type in the middle of the page.

"Tolerant."

"Oh, tolerant," she says, "I know that word."

If Cindy were to read her journal out loud to me line by line, she would catch many of the stops, and with my help be able to add, take away, and rearrange to get the sentences to make sense. This is still her main need at the re-writing stage—getting her sentences straight by reading what she has out loud. And for someone with Cindy's problems, this takes years of oral proofreading with a partner who knows how to say things clearly.

In the heat of a venting journal, Cindy still has not internalized many of these skills. Part of the problem lies at the thinking stage; my guess is that if we could mike Cindy's mind, it is spluttering out these kinds of circling half-thoughts: the medium is the message. It would have been interesting at this point to see what she might have been able to "fix" if she had proofread alone after she'd cooled down.

However, since students are told over and over that in their journals they should just let their ideas flow without any concern for "correctness," I would only talk to her about her errors if she had chosen a short section of this letter, rewritten it, and proofread it alone and with a partner

My experience is that at least half of the mistakes we note in the work of problem writers result from the inability to take what they know "in speech" to their written language and that oral proofreading over a long period of time is the best strategy for letting the student hear what they already know. Once they get so they can really hear their voices, they hear the "end-stops" and cease making so many "jumbles" in the first place. Then they are able to begin catching many of their mistakes alone. This takes years. That is why there is such a need for teachers K–12 to agree on a simple oral and silent reading revision/editing matrix that will be used consistently until these students make one of the big breakthroughs: being able to write what you can say. And I think it's best to do this training within the context of frequent short re-writings.

10
Kathy

"Mrs. H . . .Kathy . . .somebody . . .help!" Lori's voice snarls from the far side of one of the computer banks. "It won't let me type; it just keeps beeping at me."

I notice Kathy has located herself at the most remote station of the lab, a Do Not Disturb distance from the heaving and SOSs of the rest of us.

I finish helping Mike save and am heading in Lori's direction when I hear her mutter, "Never mind, never mind, I got it myself."

"How come half of my poem is gone?" Patty wants to know.

6B is experimenting with a new computer program with color, graphics, and different fonts to put together a class book of poetry, an attempt to capitalize on Christmas vacation anticipation. But for 6B, new and havoc are often synonymous.

"I know I told it to print, but nothing's happening," Robert says.

"Duh. Check the paper," Joan tells him.

Jerry has pushed his keyboard to one side so he'll have room to write by hand. I watch him carefully trace over every other line of a piece of notebook paper, using a ruler to make his dark lines perfect. "What are you up to?" I ask.

He doesn't answer, but goes on with meticulous care. When he finishes, he clips the pattern of straight lines beneath a piece of white paper. Then he begins to neatly copy one of his corrected poems.

Jerry has absolutely refused to do his poems on the computer. I can't find the letters I want. I keep losing stuff. It pisses me off. I'm not doing it, he told me as I was bringing the class down today. Round 34; and the winner is . . . Jerry. Okay, I told him, as long as you find a way to make neat copy for the class book. And no fooling around.

I see Vic is threading the paper in the printer for Robert.

Calvin motions for me to read the beginning of his Lie poem:

> *School is my most favorite place to be*
> *It is so fun to be in school I could go all*
> *year around*

Using Kenneth Koch's ideas we have done Wishes, Lies and Dreams poems as well as cinquains, haiku, acrostics—the usual assortment of poems for kids who think they won't like writing poetry. Some students, mostly the girls and Joe, have played around with other forms: short rhyming blues poems modeled after Langston Hughes, image poems after Williams' wheel barrow and plums.

It's only our second day in the computer lab experimenting with this new program and a lot of the kids are verging on frustration boil-over. But minute to minute most of us are managing to hang in there.

"Don't forget to print out a rough draft of just the words of your poem for me to skim before you do your final copy with color and pictures," I remind them over the din.

We already wrote all of the poems in the room and now they're mostly just trying to get them on the computer and printed, but as they do that they find they want to revise or sometimes they just make mistakes transposing. I quickly look through the drafts I've been given so far:

> *Love is bright.*
> *It smells like a bed of roses.*
> *It tastes like cotton candy.*
> *Love sounds like a bird singing*
> *and it feels as gentle as a summer breeze.*

Cindy Lane

> *Dreams soaring in your mind.*
> *Things that never do come true.*
> *Crashing hard to the ground.*

Patty Morgan

Such love I have for my father
I love him lying in my face
I miss when he is not by my side
I thank him for all the times
he was there for me
I love his greedy & cocky ways
How I will love him forever

No name. For a second I'm confused; then I realize it's a Lie poem. It isn't a poem I've seen before. I'm sure it's a girl's voice, but I'm struck by the fact that this might belong to any of the 6B girls: Lori, Cindy, Joan, Patty, or Kathy.

I'm standing near Kathy. She chose this same remote spot yesterday as well and has been working away without a peep both days.

"Sorry to interrupt, but is this by any chance yours?"

Kathy glances at it and shakes her head no.

"But could you look at this while you're here so I don't have to bother printing a rough draft. I'm trying to get all of these done by the end of the period. I want to spend tomorrow just putting in the pictures and doing the color."

I read over her shoulder:

Love is like a wet rat coming from the rain
   struggling to stay warm
Determined   Afraid
Honest   Scared
  Holding from each other
  the pain that you feel.

"Oh, this is so good, Kathy, and not a single mistake."

She smiles and just then across the room I see that Stan's keyboard is balanced precariously on the top of his monitor. In the cleared space he has set up a kind of obstacle course with pads and surge protectors.

"Oh me, he's using the roller ball from his mouse . . .excuse me," I whisper to Kathy and move quietly in Stan's direction.

Now I know that a few weeks ago in order to try to keep Stan on task, I would have asked Kathy to sit by him. She has been his partner many times this year for that reason. I've always counted on Kathy. Please number from 1 to 10. She would. Open to the top of page 70 where we left off yesterday. Her hand would turn the pages. When I needed to steady from the pitching of the rest of the room, I could fix on Kathy—a horizon line, a reality check. On some of the more difficult days, her sympathetic brown eyes assured me that we would all make it through to the bell.

Last spring when Kathy set up her program with our guidance counselor, he placed her in a regular English 12 class. It would better prepare her for her goal: to go to a two year community college to get an associate degree in childcare. I don't know, she told me after her schedule conference, I'm afraid I can't do it. Kathy puts forth a lot of effort, but she has problems understanding what she reads and her writing still needs a lot of one-on-one conferencing to finally become clear. I told her, why not try it, and if it didn't go well, she could always switch back to ILS.

The very first day of classes in September, there she was in the front row of 6B—her neat head nodding, her brown eyes full of belief. When I showed my surprise at seeing her, she said: English 12 was like being in a foreign country. She'd tried it first period that morning. I had no idea what he was talking about, she said. Too many big words and sentences too fast.

My first contact with Kathy was back in eighth grade when she was placed in my rowdy junior high study hall, midway through the semester. I learned later, after I got to know her in tenth grade English, that she, and her two sisters, and her mother, had fled North Carolina and that she had felt very lost and frightened in the beginning months. I was too embattled myself to connect with any of that when she first appeared.

I hadn't had an eighth grade last period study hall for years. The first week in September I ran it the way I did high school study halls: I'll be working; you'll be working; the bathroom passes are on the clipboard; be sure to sign in and out; let me know if you need anything; have a nice year. Things started to erode almost immediately: loud entry, bringing no work, being late, calling out, using the bathroom pass to wander, the hurling of objects while I corrected papers.

Thirteen-year-old civility disappears at a shockingly accelerating speed. Too late to gear down; no exits. *Lord of the Flies.* And the karma of my initial naiveté was that on the bleak November day that Kathy showed up as a new student, rather than walking into an organized community of people quietly going about their business, she came upon a pitched battle: me in front, watching their every move, to ensure that there were no infractions of the rules instituted *a posteriori.* Mutiny only a few tense inches beneath the silent surface. I barely saw this new girl, certainly gave her no warmth or welcome. I just glanced at her admit slip with one eye, while holding the group with the other, motioned her to a back table, and the only remaining chair in a room of thirty-four. She dug in as best she could and quietly worked each eighth period for the duration of the term—by which time we'd gone from hostile to grudging. On that final day in January when, thank the gods, this gang would all switch to Technology, and I had the chance to start over with a new group, Kathy lingered by the door until the rest of the kids had all burst free. She hesitated and for the first time I heard her speak, Well, goodbye, she said, smiling. I hope you have a nice evening.

In difficult situations, it's easy to exploit those students like Kathy who are docile and good. They always get placed as buffers around the troublemakers. They get asked to run the errands because you can trust they'll go and come back without making faces in the little windows of the classroom doors on the way. They get less help because they manage to go on somehow while you're giving a disproportionate amount of time to the kid who will take apart the desk, screw by screw if you don't. This was the case with Kathy in a group like ILS 6B. I could count on her and I did. Again and again and again.

This was the case in her life out of school as well. Her mother had medical problems; her younger sister was picked on by her peers; her older sister had just moved back with a baby. Kathy felt she had to take care of them all. They let her. On the other hand, some of this same willingness and need to please had taken her from being a shy, frightened eighth grader who never spoke, to being the regional president for Future Homemakers of America, a job that required having to get up and run meetings and make speeches in front of several hundred people. Good skills being practiced, but her journals spoke increasingly of feeling overwhelmed, of feeling no one listened to her, not even her boyfriend. Everyone said: Kathy is such a nice girl, so ready to drop everything and help. It's hard, with all that praise for saying "yes, yes, yes, it's no trouble at all", to learn to say "no" and "how about me?" Maybe people wouldn't still like you.

Kathy's tenth and eleventh grade journals briefly summarized bizarre childhood experiences, implied abuse. Once, when she was nine, she had been picked up by an older man at a shopping mall. No further information. A month or so ago, Kathy began to seem different. She smiled less. She didn't respond as quickly or willingly to my every directive. Oh, I thought, Kathy must be having a difficult time. One day she was even late to class and not full of concern. I was in the library. I didn't realize it was so late, she said. Make her get a late pass; you always make us get a pass, several of the students yelled.

Soon after this, I read Richard Wright's short story, "Big Boy Leaves Home" to the class. As soon as the story ended I suggested that they write a ten-minute journal, trying to remember a turning point in their lives, something that had changed them like Big Boy when he killed the white man. Kathy did not start to write for a long time. Students knew they always had the option to do free writing anytime they didn't want to use the suggested topic. That night when I read her journal, it said:

> November 30
>
> I am talking to a woman at mental health. I see her two times a week. I am beginning to talk to her about some things that happened to me when I was a kid. It is scary. She told me that for now it might be good for me to only talk about my past with her. I can even call her and talk on the phone when I remember some bad things.

I have often asked Kathy to be partners with some of the more difficult students in the class: Jerry, Mike, Stan. She'd struggle along, trying to keep them on track, refusing to be drawn into their diversions, and leaving me a little more free to give some individual help to the others. Yesterday at the beginning of the lab session I asked her if she'd team up with Stan to help him get his poem on the computer.

She said, "Can I speak to you in the hall for a minute?"

We ducked out, with me still keeping an eye on the group. Kathy looked frightened.

"What's wrong?" I asked.

"I don't want to be partners with anyone," she said. "It's tiring and it makes it much harder for me to get my work done."

"Of course," I told her. "You're right."

Today while Kathy returns to her love poem, I slip to the back of Stan's chair. Just as he's about to drop the mouse ball down his notebook ramp, I say, "Stan."

And of course Kathy *is* right and I celebrate her assertive beginning, but when the room is rocking, it will take me a while to break my habit of looking to Kathy, straight in her chair, her pencils in the tray, her paper ready.

11
Patty

Patty Morgan is rivaled only by Vance as an absentee. The line of small red *A*s that follows her name is only interrupted occasionally by a blank white square. But I haven't switched to putting down only a *P* for the one or two days a week that Patty's present. I guess this means I still have hope. For when she is here, she does some work: writes poems, logs in her reading records, occasionally speaks—usually negative critiques of that day's activity. Her red nails signal disgust, a sign that at least she's still listening, still alive enough to protest.

Patty Morgan appeared last Friday after being absent all week.

"Do you want to know what we've been doing so you can try to catch up?" I asked as she slid into the room.

"Why bother? she said. "I'm out of here soon." Her bright fingers sliced the air.

I handed her the revised drafts of her poems. "So many good ones; it seems a shame not to get them in the book."

She didn't respond, but she did look over what she'd written as she settled in her seat.

On her way out, she handed me one of her papers. "Maybe this color one," she said.

Black
Closed world
No Feelings
Nothing to care about

Just as with many of my other students, I've taught all of the children in Patty's family: one older brother and Patty's fraternal twin, Molly, and a one-year-younger sister, Ann. The three girls are all in the same grade. Molly is in my regular English 12 class, but this year Ann is living with a foster family and going to school in a nearby town.

Sometimes when I end up teaching whole families, it's interesting to note how strong the genetic stamp can be: coloring, bone structure, body rhythm, voice. That first day of class when I glance back through the rows, even without looking at the names, I can't help thinking, There's a Haney; I'll bet that's a Douglas. But the reverse is often true as well. The Morgan girls are surprisingly different; though, I think, all have the same father and mother.

Ann: fair and model slender, dressed in short skirts, ruffled sheer blouses, with changing pale hair (up, down, back, braided, sometimes all of these in one period). A maker of love collages: print and pictures cut from *Seventeen* and *Sassy* and *YM*, pasted on large pastel sheets of construction paper and turned in for extra credit in lieu of essays. Ann may not be placed near any boys since the resulting hormonal activity is hard to structure positively. And only near girls who are super secure. Otherwise there are fights—the scratching of flesh, the pulling of hair. Inappropriate epithets. Ann often assumes the role of space cadet: Earth to Ann, Earth to Ann, the students say.

Molly: large, dark, quiet. The eyes, the rhythm of a Jersey. The pretty smudged face of the kitchen maid, hidden by slattern-hair and baggy dark garments, waiting to be discovered on the backstairs of a Gothic novel. So earnest and careful in the filling in of vocabulary blanks. A maker of children's books, full of neatly crayoned suns and cottages, with smiling windows, surrounded by tulips. Her journals, thick with dark resentment—the inequities of class, her birth into such a clan. She will sit anywhere and often it is on the near side of Ann. But she prefers the back.

Patty: tall-tall, long-boned and thin. Her neutral hair always reminds me of mine in a hated picture from fourth grade: hair pin-curled by my grandmother with no consideration for what the cowlicks dictated, for the predisposition of the ends. Patty's jeans and shirt look slept on, in. Generic. Camouflaged to move unseen (except when her long red nails flutter up like startled birds.) Her countenance is fogged in and sullen. Her favorite subject, Consumer Math: the balancing of imaginary accounts, the purchase of furnishings—a bedroom suite, a Formica kitchen set, an entertainment center. Patty is a reader: V.C. Andrews and prairie stories. Starvation in attics and sudden, bitter storms that blind and lose you even in known space.

But the journals of all three girls tell a similar story: of their mother's recurring trips to psychiatric centers, of their fear of their father—his harsh authority and chronic anger, of how they live on one side of the house with their mother, while their father and brother live on the other. Of random injustice.

Patty Morgan is here again today. And on a Monday—that's very unusual.

"Well, hello," I say as she passes by.

She only shrugs. All period she is withdrawn. She doesn't have her book. She refuses any alternates.

As the class is going out the door, she says, "This is it, my last day."

"Oh, Patty . . ." Her hand raises to ward off my words. I retreat. "Where will you be going?" I ask her.

"Someplace else," she says.

And then she's gone, a line drawn through her name. It's as though she's been fading, fading so that her final blip goes unseen. After school I sort out folders. Down in the corner pocket of Patty's lean portfolio, I find a shiny silver prom program from a nearby school. On the cover, the silhouette of a man and woman, dancing before the outline of a full moon; the prom's theme in script beneath: Moonlight Magic. Inside, written in round school-girl cursive, the names of the Prom Court: Selena and Shawn, King and Queen. The 1st, 2nd, and 3rd runners-up: Tara, Duane, Zoe, Kevin, Krista, Buddy. And on the pages marked MEMORIES these notes:

- Finding out Kevin Mitchel has a girlfriend

- Glenn and Heather fighting.

- Troy Taylor getting pissed at Jill because she's dancing Danny Miller.

- Dan Bolick hitting on Jill.
- Jill telling Dan to take a flying leap.

- Leon's prom date as ugly as sin.
- Me and Chris B. dancing
- our group portrait

- Kevin giving me the eyes.

- *The look on Zoe's face when she didn't get queen.*

- *Troy headbanging with Kevin (funny)*

Is this Patty Morgan's prom program? I don't know, but as I stand reading this high school girl's memories, I imagine her long, strange journey, where she'll be going from here.

Space

12
Space

January 27: second semester. We've made the turn; the end comes into view, hazy but there: JUNE. We're in pre-countdown. Everything that happens from here on is perceived through our "short time" lens: This too is passing.

Usually around the beginning of the semester in late January, it comes to me midway through the period that we're all whirling around in our own little spaces, that nobody's knocking into anybody else, and that it has been like this for days, even in 6B. Most of the edges of resistance have finally worn away or are being accommodated by little blips: Stay clear of Lori on Mondays, grant Calvin security-blanket room during quizzes. We've read the writing on the wall; we've added and deleted what we had the strength for, and we're into "accepted-as-groked" time.

And with this ending of the Atlas segment, my shoulders let down. 1st, 2nd, 3rd, 4th period purr by. Why did I make such a big deal out of teaching? What a pleasure!

At the close of 5th period I'm still back at my desk eating my crackers and cheese, reading *The Things They Carried* for my senior class, when my next group arrives. I look up and smile benignly: Oh, is it that time already? I haven't even thought to put their folders out; there are no guide sheets on their desks. I'm not at my usual spot beside the door. After all, we know what we're doing by now.

The increasing velocity and pitch of entry: Where's my folder? . . . Am I ever sick of this school . . . Get out of my seat. Sit in your own place . . . (The crash of two desks banging together.) . . . What, are we just supposed to sit anywhere now? . . . (The slam of the door almost in Joan's face) . . . brings me back to 6B earth.

Of course by now I am in the front of the room. My shoulders are back where they're supposed to be, tensed up toward my ears. My loudspeaker is on: Incoming. Incoming. Casualties. How could

I have forgotten how important structure is for 6B? Because this structure had become such an accepted routine, I had lost sight of its significance—Security. Translation: There won't be any surprises in this space. You will not be asked to do something you cannot do and thus be humiliated in front of your peers. Someone is in charge; you will be safe. There will be limits to just how out of control you can get. It has taken months for them to finally get the routine and believe. Then today they step into the unexpected. They glare at me with accusation: Now look what you've done, their bodies say. The room is full of random motion—bees in a new bottle.

And all of this on top of other new semester changes throughout the morning.

I decide to look decisive, like this slight modification was planned. Of course I am in charge. You will soon know exactly what is going on. I step off into that place with really nothing specific in mind, other than to keep moving forward with confidence. Trust a plan will emerge.

"All right everyone pull a chair into a circle. You don't need your folders today. The class has been doing so well, that I thought we'd take a little break from our usual routine. Don't worry it isn't anything hard."

"I hate sitting in a circle. It's like kindergarten show and tell," Neal tells us, shaking his newly buzz-cut head, but he's got his desk, and is Foxhole-ready.

"I'm not doing it," Jerry says.

Most of us laugh. This remark, like the ringing of a bell, puts us back into known territory. People start dragging desks into a circle. It isn't too chaotic.

Vic comes in late. He's used to the constantly switching arrangement of the English 10 class seventh period, but he knows how differently 6B is set up and why. He pulls up a desk so he's just barely in the circle, but enough so we don't have to match wits. He looks at me from his usual ironic distance: You're going to find this was ill-advised.

We have used circles other times during the year, but it has always remained tricky, especially at the beginning.

"I thought it would be a good idea to start the new semester by doing something different." I still have absolutely no idea what that's going to be.

"You can say that again," Neal concurs. "If I have to write another journal, I'll puke."

Indeed what I had originally planned was a return to the sanctuary of silent reading and journal writing since we'd just done several active units, doing a lot of playing around with language: reading rhythmic poetry out loud, writing collaborative poems, making a class book of polished work using the computer lab before Christmas and reading and writing children's books since our return.

I take a quick scan of the group and how they've chosen to position themselves: Robert to the left of me, then on around the ring—Calvin, Jerry, Rich, Neal, Joe, Stan, Joan, Vic, reading the newspaper, and Lori to my right. Not that differently from the way I might have seated them. I am struck by how much smaller the class has become. Out of the initial seventeen, there are only ten here today. Plus two absent.

"Where is everybody?" Stan asks. I notice how his green flannel shirt has dulled, not a trace left of its first-day glow.

"Kathy had to switch to an English 12 class because she's working at the daycare center in the afternoon."

"Maybe I'll switch to another English class," he says.

I bite my tongue. "And Cindy is doing independent work with me 5th period so she can get ready to retake the U.S. History Competency Test."

"Where's Mike?"

"Absent, along with Vance."

"Oh, Vance is never here anyway," Lori says, with a flip of her shoulder and shake of her new curly perm.

And Patty is finally and officially gone. Sam never was really here since he transferred to first period right at the beginning, and Allen's squeaking shoes are but a memory.

"So what are we going to do?" Joe wants to know.

"It better not be poetry," Neal says, "or kiddie doo da."

"And not reading."

"And not writing."

They all look at me. I'm searching: different, but possible, minimum reading and writing. I feel there's about 30 seconds of open space before shut-down. A stack of play books on the shelf that I haven't used for several years grabs my eye. In it is this pretty awful student-written play, "The Rebel," which I can remember a long-ago group liking. A light goes on.

"How about if we divide into small groups and let each group make a short movie?" Do not get carried away here.

"A movie?" Jerry says, his eyes squinting with suspicion.

"How the hell could we do that?" Neal wants to know.

"The school has two cameras. Does anybody in the group have a camcorder?"

No one signals a yes.

"You mean like a made-for-television movie," Joe says. "Cool."

"Television is dumb," Rich mumbles, making one of his rare participatory discourses.

"A movie of what?" Robert says, wiggling his glasses nervously up and down on his nose.

"A soap opera," Joan replies.

"'The Young and the Restless,'" Lori says. "But where would we get the hunky actors?"

"Gluk."

"Can we take the camera out of school?" Stan wants to know.

The permutations of Stan and the school's camera equipment frame through my brain. "I'll have to check on all of that. For now think of things you could set up in or right around school, unless you know of someone who's willing to loan you a camera."

"Like how?"

"Probably we could work it out to divide into groups of three and each group could come up with its own plan, decide what kind of movie."

"X-rated?" Neal says.

I reach behind me to the recycle box and pull out a small stack of paper. I pass that around the circle.

"What's this?"

"I thought you said no writing."

"What kind of short movie do you think it would be fun to make? Something you could edit down to from ten to fifteen minutes that you could put together with two other people and show to the class. Think of the kinds of things you like to watch on TV."

"I don't watch television," Rich says.

Vic has stopped reading the paper.

"Just jot down anything—a list of ideas. Just anything that comes into your head. Then we can share some of these. You don't have to put your name on them. I'll collect them and maybe make up a list of all of the workable ideas to give to everybody tomorrow."

"Like what?'

"How long did you say this movie has to be?" Vic wants to know.

"Maybe ten to fifteen minutes, once you cut out all of the "dead wood." They are used to the "dead wood" process from their re-write-revision work.

"I hate that "dead wood" crap. Why do we have to always do everything twice?" Neal wants to know.

"Well, let's not worry too much about all that until we're a little farther along."

"Like what?"

"It could be just a part of something; you wouldn't have to do the whole thing. Like just one scene. Jot down whatever ideas come to you."

"I'd get arrested," Neal says.

But they do start to think and put things down. They confer and look at each other's papers. I notice there's only five minutes left since the classes are shortened for activity period. They keep going for a little longer. Neal and Joe and Rich are whispering and laughing.

"What girl is going to do that?" Rich says.

"Since we only have a few minutes before the bell, let's just go around once very quickly to see what some of the possibilities are. Then for homework, think of more ideas."

"We don't do homework in this class," Stan reminds me.

"Robert, you start."

"Pass," he says, with his paper face down.

We continue around the group: a mystery, pass, pass, a car chase, a western, pass, a love story, pass, about a teenage girl who runs away.

"Okay, keep thinking." I start to collect the papers. "What we'll do at first is to take a look at how TV scripts are put together; then we'll watch a few things on TV. We'll take about a week to do that. Then we'll form the groups and get started."

"Scripts?" Robert says.

"It's like a movie play. Tomorrow we'll read a script some high school students wrote."

"Did they make a lot of money?" Calvin wants to know.

"Probably not, but they had the fame of having their play in a book."

"Was it on network TV?" someone asks.

"Probably not, but . . ."

"So why bother?" Neal says. "We want a big-bucks contract before we agree to do the script."

"Yeah," Rich says, laughing.

"Do I have everybody's ideas? So tomorrow we'll read a TV play."

Only about half the class is really still with me, but I want to lay down as much of the new structure as I can before tomorrow. To somewhat defuse the possible cries of protest when they find the playbooks in the circle.

I have them put back their desks. It isn't too chaotic.

"I want to work alone," Vic tells me as he passes by.

"Let's wait and see how this all shapes up."

He rolls his eyes.

As they go out the door I hear Neal and Rich and Joe still talking.

"Yeah, but how are you going to fix it so you can blow up a car?" Rich says.

13
Props

Planning period I take a look at the script of "The Rebel" by The Monroe-Dover Tenth Grade English Class (copyright 1974.) The thin paperback anthology also includes adaptations of *Old Yeller*, "Twelve Angry Men," and "The Open Boat." But these have been abridged to the point that only the sparest of flattened plot lines link them to their original. Plus the high school play is the only one with a vocabulary level accessible to the poorer readers in 6B.

It turns out there are thirteen copies. That's some kind of an omen—just enough for all of us, even if Vance makes one of his bi-monthly visits. Plus the play is short enough for us to go through it all in one period and still have time to take a look at how the staging and camera directions are done. The plot might be appealing:

<u>Scene I:</u> A father, Mr. Martin, hassles his sixteen year old son, Ricky, about his long hair, his sloppy clothes, his grades, and the music he listens to.

<u>Scene II:</u> Ricky tells his girlfriend, Karen, he's decided to run away to California so he can be free, and Karen decides to go along because her parents have just told her she is not allowed to go out with Ricky anymore.

<u>Scene III:</u> In California Karen and Ricky have been invited to a hippie pad, where they plan to crash for a few days until they figure out what they want to do with their lives. Here they are exposed to drugs and talk of free love.

<u>Scene IV:</u> Karen and Ricky realize that the hippie life is not for them and they return to their parents who are happy to see them. The parents promise to give Ricky and Karen more freedom about things like hair styles, and the two teenagers agree to be more responsible about things like their homework.

"The Rebel," besides being easy enough for 6B to read, shows that the Dover-Monroe students knew how to begin the scenes "in the middle," either in the midst of the conflict or only moments before the setting up of tension. This will make it a good model for the 6B scripts. They can see how to "cut to the chase." Considering the 911 television and car crash movies some of the kids in 6B watch, I wonder what the class will say about the "off in the sunset" denouement arrived at by those tenth grade students more than twenty years ago. I wonder if 6B will pick up on the stereotypes.

A new 6B problem with reading a script out loud is that several of the more willing participants are no longer in the class: Cindy, Kathy, and Patty. Also we are short on girls, only Lori and Joan are left, but fortunately "The Rebel" leans heavily to male roles and the number of characters should work out well: three long parts, and seven short, plus a narrator. It's important that each member of the group has something to do. I tentatively line up who might play the major parts and hope I can cajole most of the rest of the class into taking the smaller bits.

On Tuesday when 6B starts to arrive, I am by the door and the desks are already in a circle, but I decide to wait to pass out the books until they've heard again about how a high school class got their play published, etc. Semi-magically they all get seated with minimal negotiation and pretty much where they were yesterday. The success or failure of a lesson often depends on who is sitting by whom.

I look around the circle. Mike is back. Vance is not. Mike has found a place between Joan and Vic, which should work okay. No one else is out. There is a mood of calm.

"Joe, since Mike was absent yesterday, could you fill him in on what we're talking about for the next class project?"

Joe is all business. "We're going to get into groups and make short movies."

"What kind of movies?" Mike wants to know.

"The kind they've got in the back room at Sunrise," Neal says.

Joe ignores this and continues, "Your group can decide."

"You mean like NYPD?"

"But short," Joan says. "Just one part."

"A scene," Lori tells him.

I add, "Only about fifteen minutes."

"Whose group am I in?" Mike wants to know.

And indeed where to put Mike so he'll do something productive will be a challenge.

I check the clock—always the decision: whether to push to get through what was planned or to go with what's happening. I decide to cut to the play since I don't think it's strong enough to break unfinished and come back to tomorrow.

I remind them that we won't divide into groups for a week or so. First we'll need to get more of an idea how to put together a script and how to do the filming. That today the class can get a rough understanding of what a script looks like and then the rest of the week we'll watch a few short TV programs to see how they're put together.

"What ones?"

"What are some of the shows you watch?"

They call out: "As the World Turns," "Lost," "Law & Order."

I tell them I'll pick a few different types from the ones they've mentioned. Then I go on building up to passing out the books. "If your script is good enough, your group might even get it published. Today we're going to look at a play by a tenth grade class." I start the play books round the circle." No protests. Just keep moving.

"All right, now open to page 17.

"What page?"

"Seventeen."

"What page?"

I write it on the board above my head.

"What page?"

I point to the number.

At this stage everyone but Jerry has his/her book open. He has his head down. I decide as long as he stays quiet that's as much as we can expect. I know for sure he will not take a part, but I'm hoping he will get involved once we start watching the shows and especially once we have the cameras.

I have them glance down the page to see that this simplified TV script is very much like a play, how the parts that are inside the parentheses are just directions. I draw parenthesis marks on the board and remind them that the actors don't say those parts. They are quiet so I figure they're following as much as they need to know for now.

I go on. "Okay, now see where it says 'Ricky dot dot'? That shows who is going to speak and then right after that is what he says."

"We know all this," Lori tells me.

"I knew you probably did, but I thought we might need to review it a little. All right, does everyone pretty much see how it works?"*

No one says anything.

Everyone but Jerry continues to be focused on the page. I tell them that "The Rebel" takes place back in the 1960's, pretty much the same time period as *That Was Then, This Is Now*. A sixteen year old boy and girl run away because they don't like their parents' rules.

"I can dig it, man," Joe says. Joe is the only person in the class who had listened to Cat Stevens when I once told them he was one of my favorite singer-songwriters.

I give them enough more of the plot line so they'll know where we're going: that the boy and girl go and stay with some "hippies" in California, that the play is about what they learn as a result of running away.

"I ran away once," Mike says.

"Well, then maybe after we read the script, you can say how realistic it is."

"Read?" Robert says.

"Yeah, I thought we told you 'no reading,'" Neal protests.

Performing in an unruly bar might be an invaluable part of student-teaching. And being a bouncer.

"It's short and easy, and it's just so your group will know how to write a scene. There are only a few medium-size parts. All the rest are very, very small. All right, look up at the top where it says Cast."

"I want to be the girlfriend," Joan says. She looks around with her chin out in case there are any cracks, but there seems to be nothing like that in the air.

"Good. You be Karen."

"I want to be the Hippie Girl," Lori says. "Doesn't she have a name?"

"Apparently not," I tell her.

"Well, that's dumb. When we do our play, we're certainly going to give everybody a name."

I say I agree.

"All right, now the main boy character is Ricky . . ."

"Don't give me a part," Joe says.

"Me either," Robert and Calvin mumble.

"I'll take the part of the hero," Mike says.

"Okay, Mike, you be Ricky."

Joan talks Stan into doing the part of Mr. Martin. "I'll show you where to read and whisper any words you don't know," she tells him.

Finally Robert and Calvin agree to be Hippie 2 and Hippie 3 if we'll help them.

I see Joe is busy skimming through the script, his mouth silently forming words.

"Hey," he says, "these people are smoking weed. Mary Jane."

"Yes."

Joe turns back to the beginning. "All right," he says, "I've changed my mind. I'll be this main Hippie dude. Hippie number 1."

Wow.

"Good. Now who's left? Vic, will you be the person who reads the stage and camera directions?"

"Are we getting graded on this?"

"Well, yes in the sense that it's part of the participation-process, but not on how well you read." These are Vic's terms, not mine.

"Just do the long italicized sections and the important directions in the parentheses. Not the little things like where it says 'angrily,'" I tell him.

He looks it over and nods.

"All right, who else do we need? The rest are very, very small parts."

Lori says she'll do the two mothers because it doesn't look like they ever have to talk to each other.

Stan leers at her. "That'll make you my wife."

Lori does not make a snide comment. Amazing. She's busy pulling her hair back into a more matronly do.

The girls get Rich organized to be Mr. Jones, the other father.

"Make Neal do something," Rich says.

Vic speaks up. "Neal, you read the directions for Scenes three and four."

Neal agrees and lowers his jean jacket from around his ears.

I move along as though such cooperation is an everyday 6B occurrence.

"All right, let's get started. We have just enough time to finish by the bell if we move right along. Remember to notice how all the parts look on the page."

I'm Sick of This Already

Vic begins:
> Scene I (*Early Monday Morning*)
>
> *The scene opens in the small town of Harpersville, Wisconsin. There's a long shot of a quiet, neat neighborhood. Children are walking to school. Men are going to work. Birds are singing.*

"Tweet, tweet," someone sings.
Rich looks up puzzled. "A long shot?"
"A camera shot, not a gun," Neal tells him.
Vic gives the group a cool "let's get this over with" stare.

> *The camera goes in close to a nice house and we can hear shouting. Then we cut to the living room. A tall sixteen year old boy and his medium-sized father are arguing.*

Mike comes in right on cue:

> How I wear my hair ought to be my business.

Joan pokes Stan and whispers his part to him. Stan says in a loud, authoritative voice:

> You look like something the cat dragged in.

We laugh with pleasure at how father-like he sounds. Again Joan whispers very softly. Stan continues:

> No son of mine is going to be seen on the streets . . .

Joan assists and Stan goes on.

> . . . looking the way you do.

Lori enters as Mrs. Martin:

> Yes, Ricky, your father and I agree. Your hair looks disgraceful. We want you to get a haircut today after school.
>
> Mr. Martin: And what about that terrible music you listen to?

> Mrs. Martin: And your clothes. We buy you good clothes and then you rip holes in the knees.
> Mr. Martin: And your grades have been going down.

"Bitch, bitch, bitch," someone hisses.

> Ricky: (*walking angrily toward the door*) I have a right to run some of my own life. You cannot make me cut my hair. (*He goes out and slams the door.*)

Neal says, "You tell him, Ricky boy."

> Mrs. Martin: (*opens the door and calls down the sidewalk*) You are going to be grounded unless you get your hair cut! (*She goes back inside.*)

Lori mumbles, "I don't think she'd yell out for her neighbors to hear."

> (*The camera goes up close on Mr. Martin who is sitting with his head in his hands.*)
>
> Mrs. Martin: (*quietly*) Don't worry, dear, I'm sure when he comes home from school he will have gone to the barber.
> (Fade out.)

"Yeah right," Lori says. "That's a scene?"

Jerry's head is up and he's watching the group like he's waiting to see where the little ball of speech will pop out next. Several are running their fingers down the page with the dialogue so they'll be able to come in when it's their turn.

> Scene II (*Same Morning*)
>
> (*Long shot of a suburban high school, a lot of students crowd around talking, waiting for the bell. Cut to a close up on Ricky and his girlfriend, Karen, small, with long, straight blond hair, talking.*)

"Blond. Of course blond," Lori says.

> Of course I think your parents are wrong. My parents are the same way. They just told me I can't go out with you anymore.

I'm Sick of This Already

Joan speaks in a girlfriend-voice, quiet and comforting.

I notice that Joe is out of his seat. He's doing something by the pencil sharpener. He gives me a sweet look and returns to his place with a sheet of paper folded over. We continue on through Scene II with Ricky slowly talking Karen into running away even though she feels it is impractical and dangerous. His main argument: You would if you loved me. Joe continues to be busy at his desk, but he's turned so I can't quite see what he's up to.

Neal takes over the narration. Vic reaches back and gets the newspaper from the magazine shelf.

> Scene III (*A Few Days Later*)
>
> *Camera scans a California hippie pad. Karen and Ricky are sitting on mattresses with four people who . . .*

Neal stops to watch Joe who is stealthily circling behind the group. Everyone looks up. Joe leans over between Calvin and Robert. I raise my hands for an explanation.

"We're just getting ready," he whispers to me, the soul of innocence as he tucks something in Calvin and Robert's hands. They glance down covertly and giggle. Joe returns to his seat.

I'm on the edge of knowing what's up. I motion Neal to go on.

> *Karen and Ricky are sitting on mattresses with some hippies who have long stringy hair. There are sheets on the windows and a lot of bags of trash around.*

Joe transforms to Hippie 1. He sprawls and crosses his ankles. He slows way down:

> Hey, man, want to smoke a little grass? (*reaches in his pocket and pulls out a joint.*)

I am jolted fully awake, the adrenaline of shock. For indeed Joe has reached into his pocket and brought out a fat homemade joint expertly rolled in a cigarette paper, slightly thicker in the middle, with the paper twisted a little on each end.

"Whoa," I say, rising from my desk at the same time I'm wondering what the heck I want to do with this situation.

Joe continues in his sprawl, goes on in his "hippie" voice, "Stay cool, man. What we've got here is excellent homegrown from the pencil sharpener." He points to a small mound of wood shavings on top of his desk.

I sit back down. Everyone is laughing, even Vic.

"He got you good," Neal says.

"Indeed he did," I say. "My heart is still pounding." I look at the clock. "I think if we hurry we might be able to finish this scene before the bell.

Everyone is watching Joe and grinning.

> Hippie 1: (*taking a drag and holding in his breath*)

Joe does this, then speaks without breathing.

> How about a toke, man? You look pretty uptight.

Joe passes the joint down to Mike who nervously takes a drag.

> Ricky: (*nervously*) Thanks.
> (*Karen looks on with a scared expression on her face.*)

Just then the bell surprises us.

"Cheese it; the cops," Neal says.

They start jumping up. Joe retrieves the "joints" from Mike and Calvin and Robert. Everyone is giggling and knocking about a little out of focus. I don't even think of asking them to put their desks back in rows. The room empties. Only Joe is left, just swinging his suede jacket over his shoulder.

He's still laughing. "You look a little wasted," he tells me.

"You're quite the actor," I tell him.

"You've just got to have the right props," he says, as the door closes behind him.

I sit and listen to the muffled slam of lockers, the floating voices racing to lunch. As I look around the circle, I still see their faces, still feel their electricity. Their afterimage.

And then I start to laugh, imagining how I might explain method acting to Calvin and Robert's mother on the phone.

* Play dialogue punctuation is much easier than writing and reading story conversation. The print clues of story dialogue have been very difficult for many of the students in 6B. It was by having students read novels out loud as plays in class that I discovered that many of them did not know that dialogue in a new paragraph means a new speaker. Imagine the breakdown this causes when reading silently and what problems it presents in writing personal narratives and fiction as well. It's tough to make the big leap from telling to showing without this skill. It is hard for them to remember to break and indent at the beginning of the next speech and then to understand what goes in quotations and to know how to switch to the words that would actually come out of the character's mouth. Many were forever trying to write things like "He said we should leave." Understanding that quotation marks are like cartoon bubbles helps.

14
Calvin

Calvin Brooks *Free Writing - Final Copy*
February 27

My dream of a perfect life is to have a big house. It would be a blue house with black shutters. It would have four bedrooms 3 upstairs and one downstairs for an office. The master bedroom upstairs has sliding doors that open up to a deck. The master bedroom has a king-sized waterbed and a dresser and night table and lamps that are all oak. They match. It has a full bathroom. The two other bathrooms upstairs are for the kids. The kids' bedrooms don't have everything in them. One is painted blue and one is green.

Last year at the beginning of the semester I knew that before I finished giving the opening instructions on what we would be doing that period, Calvin's hand would be in the air: I don't understand. I can't do that. I'm going to fail. Calvin was small for his age, and he always wore his faded flannel shirts tucked in and buttoned right up to his neck. His pale pinched face gave him the appearance of a little old man.

As the months passed, as he began to do all right, Calvin began to relax. His slow methodical printing, one wobbly letter at a time, speeded up. He started to understand that rough draft meant it was good to cross words out, that he could get the spelling later. After a while he could get a whole page done during writing time, and when I needed a boost, I'd read his journals—so innocent and full of plans. He started smiling from time to time and even tried little ironic remarks occasionally like saying, I can see you are feeling in a good mood today, when it was clear I was near melt-down. He made me laugh. It sure is good to have you in this class, I'd tell him and he'd grin.

All of his listening quizzes and class responses indicated that Calvin had a lot of difficulty following meaning beyond the "what just happened" level. He especially had trouble remembering who was who, so he didn't seem to be able to bring forward past actions and generalizations for the characters in the stories. This was also true for the movies. By the end of *Dead Poets* the characters of Neal, Knox, and Todd had all run together in his mind. They all look alike, he said. What we did Tuesday was gone from his memory when we started to work again on the next part of the lesson on Wednesday.

But he was almost never absent. He was never late. He always had a pencil. He gave everything we did his full effort, his thin face tight with concentration, his brown eyes squinted behind his horn rimmed glasses. He bobbed his head as he followed along.

After a while I began to think of him as "willing, but slow." Fine. He was progressing an inch at a time. He was gaining confidence. He had good work habits. He was a nice person. I thought it likely he'd find his niche and make someone a valuable employee one day.

His earnest ways did sometimes draw occasional jeers from Neal and Rich. Calvin always reported these to me immediately in the expectation that I would protect him. Usually a few days of letting him change his seat defused their need to tease him. It was important to deal with any messing with Calvin early because if it continued, Robert, Calvin's older brother, would rush to his defense, and then the whole thing would escalate: Puffing chests, meet me after school, beat the shit out of you bravado would break through whatever we were trying to do.

About once a month last year Calvin's mother called me at school. I knew the family had come through a difficult separation and divorce from a father who was abusive. Robert has been in ILS for going on his third year and his journals for the last two years had spoken of a father who was exacting beyond reason and of relief when the court finally denied the father contact with the family.

Calvin and Robert's mother was concerned about how her sons were going to make out in the demanding world of work. I sympathized. But after the first half-hour-long end-of-the-day call, I began to listen with the phone tucked between my shoulder and ear while I straightened desks, collated the next day's stories, erased boards, glad for a long cord. She wanted me to get Calvin and Robert's reading and writing up to grade level. What was their level as of right now? She kept after them at home, she said. I commended her efforts. I told her of their steady progress, their hard work, and positive attitudes, what nice people they were. You must feel good about that, I said. Would I test them and call her about their grade levels? I said I would arrange to have that done, but I thought she might consider the fact that they were making progress the important thing. She said to call her as soon as I had the results. I did. Calvin's overall reading level: 6.1, Robert's 5.7. We both felt discouraged, me even more than their mother because I was pretty certain those scores were considerably above where they were actually functioning in terms of really "getting it." A conclusion that I saw no benefit for any of us in sharing.

Calvin was absent yesterday so today as soon as the BOCES bus returned he came in to make up the journal he'd missed. He wrote with concentration for about fifteen minutes, then he handed me his paper.

The Kind of Car I Whant

> The kind of car I whant is a chevy camero. Its got to be jet black with red interier. Six silender five speed with stereo caset player. Its going to have good year tires on it and bucket seats. Then Im going to atlantic city to go swimming in the big ocean. Then Im to drive around and look at all the stores. sleep in a nice Hotel. Ill take pete with me. he and I will go around and find him a nice woman. he is going to ask the woman out and take her to get something to eat and ask her to go to his Hotel room.

Since there was time before the bell, he read his paper out loud and was able to catch many of his missing capitals letters. With a little prompting he went back and put in his missing apostrophes. As he was getting himself organized for 6B, his folder out of the box, his paper and pencil ready, I remembered Calvin's mother's concern about his future. I asked him what he wanted to do after he graduated. He said he wanted to be a security officer at the big insurance office in town. He was taking that course at BOCES. He said he hoped to get an apartment above the pizzeria. Just one room to start, with a brown stove and refrigerator in a little nook at one end. Big enough for one person, he said.

15
Robert

Robert needed longer runways. To take in the directions, to think about how to begin, to actually read or form the words, to keep returning to gather up meaning again. He needed frequent contact with the tower after takeoff: to get back on course, to revise the targeted destination. Reading or writing: Robert needed more time. He met this need by returning to the class as soon as he got his lunch tray any day he hadn't finished the assigned task during 6B. He worked with his sandwich in one hand and his pencil in the other. Usually, with some modification of the requirements, he was caught up by the beginning of the next period.

In school and out Robert was a worker. He had a job doing farm chores and milking. This involved getting up by four, and then working again until seven or eight every day after school. His family needed the money; he wanted the responsibility, he said. Though his boss picked Robert up and dropped him back off at home in the morning, sometimes he would have to get to school on his bike because he had to change from his barn clothes and shower and he would miss the bus. Yes, his mother told me on the phone, she was glad that Robert worked so hard in school and on the farm, but did I know that he hadn't been able to read the label on one of the bottles, and he'd given a cow the wrong thing and it had almost died. I suggested some strategies he might use when he couldn't figure out something important at work. She suggested that I teach him to read. Now. She said at Grantsville Central, a neighboring school district, the students completed a series of workbooks. I told her I thought Robert was making good progress. She said they began at the beginning and worked their way through to the end.

Sometimes if Robert finished his work before the lunch period was over, he leaned against the bookcase near my desk and we talked. He told me he wanted a car very badly, but he kept failing the driving test. No, not the written one. They read that out loud to him and after a few tries he'd passed. The actual out on the road test was the problem. He kept forgetting to look or signal or stop. He said his mother would not take him out enough to practice in traffic, to parallel park, to get his confidence up. He said he didn't care what kind of car or how old, just something safe that would keep going. But he didn't know how he'd ever save enough to buy one even if he did make it through the test.

Robert was in love and he used to ask my advice as to how to approach the girl he watched from afar. Like most of us, Robert's appearance improved with familiarity. His nice smile and sincerity took over, but at first meeting he was at a disadvantage. His large eyes behind bottle-thick glasses appeared frog-like, and his pudginess, especially around his middle, made me fear rejection from a teenage girl. Plus the girl he liked was a few years older. I identified with the girl, the being asked out by someone you hadn't sent any signals to. I counseled him to be alert to some signs of interest on her part before rushing in. He asked what kind of signs? I said wasn't there some girl in his church or one of his classes that he could get to know as a friend and then move on from there? He said he thought that was a good idea and he'd look around with that in mind.

Like Calvin, Robert had made gains, inch by inch by inch through difficult terrain, learning language clues that helped him decode what looked to him like secret messages. And in what now felt like hostile territory. He'd gotten so he could write half a page in a journal between the regular ten minutes in class and some added time during lunch. Usually he wrote in a voice that was dead serious, moving from one part of his day to the other, the way he walked, slow and close to the wall.

Still he'd come a long way from the beginning of last year when he'd chosen the option of not seeing *The Hustler* with the rest of the class because his church did not believe in gambling. When he mentioned some of the programs he and his family watched on television, I wanted to press him to reconsider, but I didn't.

As part of his alternate assignment, I set him up in the computer room to work on some daily free writing. He was to write for fifteen minutes and then to read back over what he had written to make it better by adding specifics, and then he was to try to correct any mistakes he saw. I knew this was ambitious, but this was the process we were trying, week after week, year after year, to internalize. Each day Robert assured me he was getting somewhere. Of course it was a hole in the plan that I didn't insist on a hard copy at the close of each period. At the end of the week when I printed Robert's file so I could go over his writing with him, I watched with amazement as the printer typed out one word: TRAPPING before ejecting the otherwise blank page. One word? One week? What happened? I asked him. I wrote more, he said, but it kept not being right so I kept pressing the key that gets rid of it.

Half a page in twenty minutes was definitely a leap from one word in five periods, but he still wasn't able to connect with his center of gravity, his heart, whatever it is that gives us that jolt of being alive. Since his speech was pretty flattened out and spare as well, it didn't help to tell him to write like he talked. Until he found a way to turn on the color, the sound, to get his experience moving and speaking, his words would just continue to march dutifully across the page.

Mid-February, and his third year in ILS, it definitely felt like some new approach was needed to shake Robert loose, so yesterday at lunch before he started his journal, I moved over to the desk next to his. I said, "Did you ever steal anything?"

I saw his body jump, his face tighten a little.

I told him, "I used to steal candy from a woman named Melba who rented a room from my grandmother." He leaned a little my way. "After school I used to sneak in while she was working at the airplane factory, slide the bottom drawer of her dresser open, and grab whatever was on top. Sometimes it was a Hershey Bar. Sometimes it was Joe Palooka bubble gum. There was a little pile of stuff, but I'd only take one thing."

Robert squinted. "How old were you?"

"About seven. It was during the war when bubble gum was really hard to get."

"You did it more than once."

"Yes. I'd grab something, push the drawer in, tiptoe to her door and peek out into the hall to make sure my grandmother or any other roomers weren't around. Then I'd quick slip up the stairs to my little room in the attic. Slowly I'd eat the candy. When I was done, I'd push the wrapping under the mattress. Then I'd whisper to myself, I'm never going to steal anything ever again."

"But then you would."

"Yes, in three or four days, I'd begin to think of that drawer, my mouth would start to taste Hershey Bar, and I would find myself slowly turning the knob to Melba's room."

Robert's eyes narrowed and he lowered his voice. "Did you ever get caught?"

"Weeks and weeks went by. The wad of papers under my mattress got bigger and bigger. Then one day... What do you think happened?"

Robert's eyes got round and he laughed. "Your grandmother found all those candy papers."

"Yes, there she was sitting on my bed with all those wrappers piled up beside her when I got home from school. She had that thin-lipped look."

"What did she do?"

"She made me spread each of them out and count them up."

"How many were there?"

"The top of a twin bed full."

"Then what did she do?"

"She made me go down with the whole stack of wrappers in a box and apologize to Melba."

Robert's body contracted. "Oh," he whispered.

"Melba said, 'I'm disappointed that you would do such a thing. If you had asked for the candy, I would have been happy to share it, but I'm glad you had the courage to come and tell me.' Now that I think about it, I figure my grandmother and Melba had gotten together and kind of rehearsed how to teach me the best lesson."

"Nobody hit you? Your father didn't use his belt?"

"No, my parents were divorced. My father lived far away in Savannah, Georgia."

"What about your mother?"

"She worked as a nurse and she didn't usually get home until after dark. She wouldn't have let anybody hit me."

"What did your mother say when your grandmother told her?"

"She made me give my twenty-five cents weekly allowance to Melba every Friday for what seemed like years."

"Years?"

"Well, probably it was only a month. You know how time is when you're a kid."

"Yeah," he said. Then he scooted down and leaned back and crossed his boots. "I stole something once."

"You did?"

"Me and Jimmy Lawson stole a pack of Camels from their hired man."

"How old were you?"

He looked at the ceiling. "Sixth grade."

"How did you do it?"

"He . . . Lem Baxter, he was an old guy who always talked to himself. He was in the barn shoveling cow shit . . ." Robert hesitated.

"Yeah," I said.

"His jacket was hanging on the hook by the door. Jimmy reaches around when Lem's back was turned . . ."

As Robert went on with his story, whenever he faded to black and white, distant camera summary, I'd ask a "go in closer" question: Where were you? Then what did he say? etc. When he was done, I asked him a few more questions; then I listed what I remembered as the key images of the incident. Robert worked it out to go on with the story down in the resource room the next period. He was to follow the cues from the list, with the help of Mr. Michaels anytime he broke down.

At the end of the day Robert brought me a neatly written final draft with his rough copy stapled to the back.

"Listen," he said.

And in that voice that is Robert's part in the chorus of this planet along with the rain, brook, cat, train, he read:

> *February 23*
> *One summer just before I went into sixth grade down at the big school, me and Jimmy Lawson were throwing rocks at the windows of an old car back behind their barn. Out of nowhere Jimmy says, Let's steal some cigarettes. I don't remember what I said, but the next thing*

you know, there's Jimmy reaching around the barn door, putting his hand down in Lem Baxter's jacket. Lem Baxter was their hired man. He was always mumbling and cussing to himself. Anyway his back was to us because he was shoveling sh__. Jimmy grabs out a pack of Camels. We took off up the hill going as fast as we can run. I was so scared Lem Baxter was going to step out and see us I almost ____ you know what. Then it turned out we didn't have any matches so we just took turns rolling the pack up in our T-shirt sleeve. We walked back and forth, being cool and laughing so hard my stomach hurt. We hid the Camels under a rock. But we never went back. Maybe Jimmy went up there some other time and lit up. But I doubt it. I'll bet old Lem's still cussing and wondering where his cigarettes got to.

16
Mike

The hopeful sputter of life that Mike exhibited as the hero in the hippie play soon fizzled. Extrapolating from the level of production for the first three quarters, it seemed likely that we would have the pleasure of each other's company for a repeat of tenth grade next year.

Mike's writing folder for the first thirty weeks of school contained three pieces of paper. The first one had a full heading done perfectly, but the rest of the sheet was blank. I remembered watching him work for twenty minutes, off and on, to get down these half dozen words. His first name and the phrase, *I'll never forget the time I* were printed on the second sheet, and the third piece contained the single word "The" with the right hand corner torn off to make a spit wad.

In class Mike was like a weak battery in February: I put the key in and maybe the engine turned over once, twice, but he never caught, never vra-vra vroomed. But he was capable of speed over long distances. Some 7th periods I saw his long-limbed body sprint down School Hill to get home and back in the 32 minute lunch period. He was a cross-country runner in a neighboring town where he lived with his father the first part of last year before he transferred here to stay with his mother.

Like Stan, Mike was also in my remedial lab class last year. He was always dressed in the latest: bib overalls, one strap undone; pump up Nikes; watches with exchangeable bands. Just like this year, he was able to go for entire periods, weeks, without doing anything (other than long trips to the bathroom). The only thing that disturbed his passivity was an offer of help; any kind of pressure to produce caused hostile hyperactivity. Mike's production range: idle or stall.

I conferred with his teachers. They threw up their hands and showed me the rows of empty boxes that followed his name in their grade books. They all said: He does nothing out of class; he does nothing in class. Unless you want to count the emission of background static: humming, pencil tapping, foot bouncing. Running to the revolutions of a different engine. They said every now and then a random question caught his attention and he called out the correct answer. His consciousness and a moment in class occasionally connected to produce combustion.

In the lab last year, for weeks, I tried every strategy I could think of to help him with his writing, with his back work since he was failing every class. To no avail.

Once he said he was a Stephen King fan so I encouraged him to find a King book of his choice in the school library. He returned before the end of the period, bearing a thick volume. He put it on the desk in front of him and said he would start it at home. He sat looking into space for the remaining ten minutes. As he left, I suggested he bring the book to lab each day. Wouldn't it be good to have something interesting to do? I never saw the book again. The only trace of the event was our librarian, Emma Lowe, appearing in my room once a week for the next month after the due date, reminding, cajoling, remonstrating. Her mouth thin with exasperation. Eventually she stopped coming. Months later every time I was getting something from the library, eyes heavenward she would bemoan the loss and sigh.

Mike seemed happiest looking at ads in the magazines, the inserts in the Friday newspaper, and that is what he did for the rest of the lab year when I finally gave up.

Soon after second semester started, one gray February ILS period, frenzied with frustration after listening to Mike on idle yet another forty-two minutes, I yelled at him from the front of the room, "MIKE, YOU ARE DRIVING ME CRAZY."

His body jolted; he grabbed up his pencil and flipped open his book. Then the bell rang. I berated myself all the way home. How could I have screamed like that?

Before homeroom the next morning I caught up with Mike in the hall. He looked a little apprehensive at my approach. I said, "I want to apologize for yelling at you yesterday. That was wrong of me."

"No, no," he said, "you were right. I'm going to start doing all of my work."

Since it wasn't too far into the semester, we talked about the possibility of him switching into my regular tenth grade English class. I said I thought he might do better in a class where the students didn't fool around, that it would call forward his more mature self. That adjustments could be made as long as he was working hard and putting forth effort.

Mike was enthusiastic. We went to see our guidance counselor, Joe Marsh. We arranged for Mike to start in the 4th period class the following day and to change to an afternoon session at BOCES.

The next day when Mike arrived, I put him beside students who might help him, a place where he wouldn't be distracted. A place just within my periphery where his random motion would not distract me.

Luckily we were just beginning a high focus unit: learning how to write a literature essay by tracing Todd Anderson's quest in *Dead Poets Society*, a movie ILS had really liked last year. The tenth grade class had already taken notes from an essay about the quest archetype: the call, the meeting of challenges, the return. The class had already read and discussed several stories as examples of the quest pattern: Wright's "Big Boy Leaves Home," Boyle's "Greasy Lake," and Faulkner's "Barn Burning."

Right away I could see that Mike was caught by the film along with the rest of the class. You know it's real when everyone gets there on time, is in their seats by the bell, and several say, Let's go. O the pleasure of sitting with a group of students when they are fully engaged.

At first Mike did a lot of calling out in response to the film. I talked to him about this at the end of class. How of course he could spontaneously laugh, but that his voice interrupted the dream of the movie, that it took us out of the world of the story. I said it was bad enough that we had to break up the film into 35 minute pieces over four days which already ruined some of the intensity. He was listening and the next day he did it less, and the third day not at all.

The discussion of the movie was lively. Many were adamant that Neal's death was all the father's fault, how Neal was the victim. Using the quest theme—that we must face and fight our dragons—most of the class finally reached a consensus that Neal was ultimately responsible because he failed to stand up to his father and that the movie was flawed in that it tended to stereotype Mr. Parry, rather than bring him forward as a complex character. Mike didn't say a lot, but it was clear he was involved. He even turned in an end-of-the-movie response sheet, rating *Dead Poets* a 5 for excellent and saying how much he hated Neal's father, how cool he thought Mr. Keating was.

Then we were down to the hard part: writing the essay. Students were given the option to use a frame that set up the introduction and provided little bridges from one part of Todd's quest to the next. They were also given scene by scene notes that would help them recall specific support for Todd's development. After an overall discussion, students worked in small groups of three to outline their generalizations and support.

I could see Mike was struggling, but he was with two strong students and they were taking the time to let him copy their outlines as they emerged. Three class days were going to be given for the first draft, revision, and editing, with additional time out of class if needed. Students could keep checking back in with their partners. Final drafts were to be done at home. I figured if Mike ended up finding the essay structure of generalization and support too difficult, he could simply write a good critical analysis summary of what Todd was like at the beginning, the turning point scenes, and what he was like by the end. This was an option I would offer to any student who was getting mired by integrating the quest motifs.

On the day the class was to begin the first draft, Mike appeared late without either pencil or paper. As soon as everyone was working, I sat with him to show him how he could feed his outline into the frame. It became immediately clear that the task was too complicated. The notes he had copied from his partners hadn't become "his." So acting as his secretary, I helped him pull out specific examples of Todd's behavior for a critical summary. He was able to remember most of the turning points and though he was often not able to generalize what these behaviors might imply, with a little guidance he could connect to those as well.

As I worked with him, I noticed that he seemed tired, that he didn't look quite right, that one side of his face was puffy. I mentioned this and he said he wasn't feeling good and that his glands were swollen.

The next day when I looked over at Mike soon after the period started, I saw that he was sleeping, his head propped between his two hands. I was busy helping students all period, but when I spoke to him briefly at the end, I saw that his neck and the side of his face were even more swollen. He said he was going to the doctor.

Mike was out the rest of the week. Except for a few students the class had reached the final draft stage of the process. We had lollipops to celebrate.

The next Monday Mike's brother Jason stopped in. He was full of excited news: That lucky dog. He's got mono. The doctor says he'll be out for weeks. He has to have a tutor.

I put together a simple day by day plan: daily journal writing, daily reading of a book of choice with brief summary notes and responses for each reading session plus a record of pages. I sent the plan to the guidance office with a stack of easy reading books in case Mike didn't have anything at home: *The Contender*, King's *Four Seasons*, *Chocolate War*, *Hatchet*. The directions said Mike should begin as soon as he felt well enough.

No completed assignments appeared. When I checked with guidance and phone calls were made home, it was all vague. Canceled sessions with the tutor, doing other work, etc. Sometimes on my way home I would catch sight of Mike turning the corner on his bike, popping wheelies in front of the Victory Market.

About four weeks later Mike did return. He had not completed any of the alternate work. Guidance arranged special help during his study hall. Nothing ever got finished. We were now reading *Macbeth* in the tenth grade class. Mike was lost and bored. He returned to some of his 6B behaviors: humming, tapping his pencil, calling out. The students around him gave him looks; they complained. Then he started going to sleep soon after the period began, his arms folded across his desk to cushion his head, his jacket pulled over his ears and mouth.

We were careful not to disturb him.

17
Joan

Getting up in the dark, a week of subzero temperatures, same old rut: school, homework, sleep, school. We are all sick of it.

I go to an after-school workshop set up by our regional English teachers' group. Transfusion time. A middle school teacher and five of his eighth graders drive six hours to do this presentation on getting students excited about writing. The teacher is on fire. The students read us some of their work, pieces full of voice and image. They are bursting with the confidence and power that comes from being engaged—real learning. The students divide us up into small groups and talk to us about their process. They read to us from their process journals: what they went through and how they felt about various stages of particular polished manuscripts in their portfolios.

Wow! This is what 6B needs. All of my students. Me.

One of their ideas sounds especially dynamic: Give each student a large brown envelope to begin a Personal Time Capsule. Have them write a Letter to Self over several weeks using a guide sheet of ideas. Guarantee that no one but the writer will read the contents (including the teacher). Add to the time capsule each year. Include other items such as CDs and DVDs, photos, artwork, etc. Seal. Present the envelopes to the students as part of a graduation rite, such as a dinner or school party. Have each student decide when he/she wants to break the seal to look back: Open in the year 2012. Or have those who want to, bury them in a leak proof vault to dig up at their twentieth reunion.

What a super activity. I go home from the workshop and adapt a guide based on the handout.* Then early the next morning I go into school to set up the unit: 12 copies of the Letter To Self guide sheets, stapled together comp paper, each packet placed in a large brown envelope. Everything's ready for 6B.

During my planning period as I put an envelope on each of the

6B student's assigned desks, I notice it has snowed. When did that happen? I look down on the parking lot. The cars are layered with several fleecy inches. The graffiti on the blacktop and the dirty gray-brown banks are gone.

The bell rings and I stand by the door. As they ricochet in, my barometer registers increased pressure—not the best day to start a new unit. Too late now.

"Look at it outside," some of them say.

Half of them go straight to the windows.

"The roads look bad."

"They better be sending us home early."

I just stand up there.

"What the heck are these?" Neal says, holding his envelope at arm's length as though it is diseased.

"Whatever it is, I'm not doing it," Jerry says and tosses his envelope onto the storage shelf under his desk.

Several students—Joan, Lori, Calvin, and Joe—are already pulling out the contents. The people at the windows amble toward their seats—Vic, Robert.

I notice that Rich and Stan are absent. I'll have to remember to go through the unit plan with them when they get back.

"Time . . .Cap . . .," Joe reads. He's wearing his suede jacket, with only a few tips of the marijuana leaf imprint on his T-shirt exposed. Provocative, but not enough to get sent by the principal to his gym locker for more appropriate attire.

"Per-son-al Time Cap-sule Pro-ject," Robert says, hitting each syllable.

"Project," Joan corrects him quietly.

By this time almost everyone has started to pull the sheets out.

"Letter to Self," Joan reads. I see she has returned her hair to its original color—brown—and she has it pulled up with a banana clip.

"Why would I write to myself? That's stupid," Neal says.

And very low someone else says, "No fucking way." Low enough that I don't have to notice it.

More grumbling, but I can see that a few of the better readers are skimming the sheets.

Joan flips to the back. "Cool," she says.

"What is this?" Robert asks.

I sit down on the stool at the podium as if we've got all day. "Before we go through this new unit in more detail, is there anyone in class who's figured out enough to give us the gist of what this project's about?"

"The gist? The gist?" Robert says.

Joe lifts his hands as though he is conducting an orchestra. "I saw a bunch of people on television put some things in a time capsule. Stuff that would really show what the Twentieth Century was all about."

"Like what?" Neal wants to know.

"Like . . .I don't really remember, but you know stuff that shows our civilization . . .like a picture of Elvis Presley."

"Or like a CD of Metalica," Robert says.

"Yeah, then people in the year 3000 dig the box up and say, What a bunch of weirdoes. Kind of like us digging up the Egyptian mummies." Joe checks to see if they're getting the concept.

"I'm not burying any of my CDs," Jerry says.

"Oh, you don't even have any CDs," someone responds.

"What we're going to do," Joan tells them, "is write anything we want to about ourselves and put it in the envelope and no one but us is going to read it. And then in like twenty years you can open it up and see what you were like when you were a teenager."

This is the longest speech Joan has ever made. The class turns in her direction.

Lori whispers, "I like your hair like that."

Joan smiles and busies herself getting out her pen.

"You can put in stuff like pictures," Calvin tells us.

"I'm not putting in any pictures." Jerry puts his head down like he's going to take a nap.

"Let's start," Joan says, "We've only got twenty minutes left."

"If you aren't going to read it, how are you going to know what we do? How are you going to grade it?" Vic wants to know.

I explain a little more and tell how the work will be evaluated. I tell them tomorrow we'll go through the sheets more fully, but for now just to pick the first topic that interests them or make up their own. To imagine they're writing to themselves when they're a certain age. I tell them to draw a little symbol on the flap that will mark it as theirs and to close the flap with the fasteners and put them in the box with their symbols facing out at the end of the period.

Joan is already writing. "I'm beginning," then she holds her paper up and reads to the class: 'Dear Me when I'm 30 years old.'"

"I'm never going to be that old," someone says.

And so the Personal Time Capsules begin. Some spend the rest of the period working on their symbols: Neal and Robert. Jerry continues to "sleep." Several are off and almost done with one side: Joe and Lori. Vic is getting his "minimum" done. Calvin is contemplating the ceiling. When I approach him, he tells me he's thinking about how he wants to start.

Joan has already begun her second page. She shakes her fingers from time to time to bring the blood back to her hand. At the end of the period she gives me her envelope, "I want you to read what I've got so far," she tells me. "Then close the flap tight."

Joan was out the first three months last year. She was having a baby. At fourteen. I tried to imagine myself at fourteen with a child. I couldn't. When the baby was about a week old, still scary small and wrinkled, I saw Joan showing her to a few junior high girls in the hall. I remembered my two sons at that age, my anxieties, my fatigue at getting up in the night. Who got up with this baby?

Once Joan returned to school last year, she continued to be out often, sometimes two or three days in a row. She had reasons: My baby has an ear infection; my mother had to go to Binghamton, so I had to stay home and take care of my baby; my baby was sick and I had to take her to the doctor. I would give her a list of back reading and journal assignments and she would slowly chip away at them during her resource room help each day.

Joan has noticeably bucked teeth and several kids in the class used to put her down. She handled this by giving back in kind. She had one friend in class last year, another outcast, and they buddied up for all the partner work. Occasionally her journals would contain phrases that showed her low esteem. Once she said, If you are ugly like me . . . Occasionally she mentioned a boyfriend. She always wrote twice as much as anyone else in the class: large, looping words about her daughter, about anything I suggested. Last year she used no periods or capitals or paragraphing. The stories were rambling and disjointed.

June of last year Joan had been out most of the week when one day she appeared in the doorway between classes. She needed to pick up her folder to take home to do some of her work. She was carrying an infant on her hip: pink-cheeked, blue-eyed, round, a curly-headed blond. An unusually beautiful child. Here she is. This is my baby, Rebecca, she said.

At the close of school I put Joan's brown envelope on top of the stack of papers I push into my book bag. I want to read her Letter to Self first, before I start to bog down. Later, at home I pull her sheets out.

> March 7
>
> Dear Me when I am 30 yrs. old. Here's what I'm thinking about when I'm 15.
>
> Me, Now: My hopes are to move back to tennise where I used to live before I moved up here to New York.
> My other hopes are to get a job as a cook or baby setter. but any job will do for me.
> My fear's are one day I weak up and my bady isn't brething and end's up dieing on me because I have a nethew that died when he was only 1 year's old so that makes me feel a little bad because Rebecca and him are only 2 mouthes apart that's all.
> My dreams are one day I will own a horse and a nice car to go with. but what I really would like is a house with a 12 foot deep pool with it.
>
> and live with my boyfriend or houband and spical live with my dauter. If I get married by then I'm surposs to get marrid in a year if then

* Personal Time Capsule Project

Over the next few months you are going to write a long letter to yourself to seal in this envelope and to open and read sometime in the future. NO ONE else but you is going to read this letter unless you want them to.

> I. Ideas for Letter to Self (Due_____)

Suggested Five Parts:

ME, NOW: my hopes, fears, dreams, intentions, goals, problems, concerns, likes, dislikes, joys, frustrations; what I like about myself; what I'm proud of; things I think about; who I am, etc.

MY WORLD: a description of my home, bedroom, school, neighborhood, town, favorite places to go, chores, allowance, pets, possessions, clothes, religion, current events that concern me; Favorites: books, music groups, movies, TV shows. Include a map of your territory.

WHAT I DO: my hobbies, pastimes, sports, school activities; what I do on weekends and vacations; special activities I do; organizations I belong to, etc.

PEOPLE IN MY LIFE: my family, my friends, my teachers, the opposite sex, "Him" or "Her," my best friends, people I'd like to know better, people I admire and respect, important people in my life, etc.

MY FUTURE: predictions; what I want to do; my long range intentions; what I'm looking forward to; my goals, hopes, and fears for the world, the rest of this year, high school, college, marriage, employment, etc.

In doing the "Letter to Self" (LTS), you do not have to write about each sub-topic. Write about what is important to you. You should write at least a page for each part. You may also want to write about something important to you that isn't mentioned. Create your own categories. This LTS is for you and it should deal with the things that are important and real in your life—"the good, the bad, and the ugly." The more honest you are, the more you will value your letter in the years to come. (Remember no one will read your LTS except you and those people you choose to share it with.)

II. Polished Writing Collection and Class Anthology:

Using some of your LTS fragments or any other ideas, write three polished writings in three different modes (see below). One will be due at the end of each of these months: March, April, and May. Plan to put at least two in the class anthology. You may also want to put your polished pieces and a copy of the anthology in your time capsule.

____poem ____memoir ____short story ____opinion essay
____play
____description ____biographical sketch ____interview write-up
____other

III. Other Ideas for Time Capsule:

____1. Make a movie with a few partners of people, places, and things around school and town that you want to remember in the years to come.

____2. Make a CD of favorite songs, friend interviews, jabber from lunch/locker/homeroom, comments from adults you want to remember, etc.

____3. Put in pictures of people and places you want to remember.

____4. Put in a copy of favorite poems, song lyrics, sayings, etc.

____5. Write notes and letters to other people in the class or school. Place them in their time capsule (with their permission).

You will be given class time off and on for the next three months. You will be evaluated on the basis of meeting the 5 page minimum (proven by noting amount completed on this guide/record sheet each work-time & a final "count out" of total pages witnessed by the teacher at the close of the unit. Extra credit will be given for additional material. You will be graded separately on each of the polished pieces. You will be part of the evaluation process.

Note: At the end of the unit your envelope will be secured for safe and private keeping and passed on to your next year's English teacher for further entries.

(* The idea and Part I taken from Ross M. Burkhardt, Shoreham-Wading River Middle School.)

18
Rich

Calvin interviewed Rich and then wrote a brief biography:

March 23

Rich Spencer was born in Stanton. He has lived all of his life up on Tanner Hill. He has four older brothers. His family has traveled to Grantsville and Clinton. The farthest he's ever been is twenty-two miles. He and his parents live in a trailer on thirty acres. He does not have any favorite TV programs. He never watches TV. They do not have a TV. He doesn't want a TV. He likes to hunt and trap and clean his guns. He does not like to come to school.

In ILS Rich is somnolent. When called on, he slowly returns, first with a dreamy smile and then with a few inaudible words. What? several of us say, leaning toward him, and though he speaks again, we still cannot hear. Every now and then life stirs in Rich's long, thin frame: when Neal is telling a dirty joke, when he can connect with the topic of guns, trapping, deer.

Once in an individual reading conference after he was supposed to have read an article on beavers as part of a progress evaluation, I began asking him comprehension questions. He said he didn't really read the words; he just looked at them and turned the pages. He already knew about beavers. He watches them lots of evenings up on his neighbor's land. The beavers have already put ten acres of the man's property under water. When beavers have taken all the trees near the edges, they have to keep damming up more so they can make the water go to the next part of the woods. Rich said he told his neighbor he'd shoot some of them for him if he wanted, but the neighbor's from the city and he said he couldn't kill innocent creatures. Rich's father told him that he better think of putting his house up on stilts pretty soon then. City people, Rich said with a laugh.

I said, Well, let me go ahead and ask you these comprehension questions just to see how you do without the reading. Rich knew almost all the answers and more: how beavers build and repair their dams, when they mate and how they raise their young, what they use their tails for, when they molt, how their lives change with the seasons. The only answer he did not know was the meaning of the word "castoreum" and how castoreum was used. I showed him how to find the answer by locating the italicized words in the reading: *an oily, brown, odorous substance obtained from the glands in the groin of the beaver and used in perfume as a fixative and at one time used to form castors in cure-all medicines.* Rich asked me questions about this, enough to see if there was any market in beaver groins; then he told me in detail what a beaver's body looks like when it rots.

The next day Rich brought in a set of beaver teeth: two, three inch gleaming ivory curves about a quarter of an inch wide. The first inch of each of the teeth was yellow-white and razor sharp, the other section, striated, alternating umber and cream. We crowded around his desk.

"They're so long," someone said.

Joan reached out and Rich placed the teeth carefully in her palm. The teeth passed around the group; everyone running their fingers gently along the edges, expressing varying degrees of wonder—all except Jerry who already "knew" beavers.

"All of this," Rich said, pointing to the long striped section, "goes back into their upper jawbone. Beavers have to gnaw. If they don't gnaw . . ." holding the teeth up to his own mouth, Rich showed how they would keep on growing, cutting through the mouth to lock the beaver's lower jaw. As he did this, his face took on a Dracula-grin. Several of us pulled back and added laughing squeals.

For the rest of the period while we read "Split Cherry Tree" (for which the beaver teeth were indeed a serendipitous anticipatory set), Richard's eyes stayed focused in the "now"; his body remained alert. How to pump that much adrenaline into his system every day?

But I'm not sure it's even possible to come up with a school program that can connect with Rich enough to keep him in school once he reaches sixteen. Rich's future goals differ from those written about in the English 10 journals. In their journals most of the English 10 students say they plan to attend college after graduation to become accountants, nurses, teachers, lawyers, music therapists, etc. Rich dreams another world altogether:

March 3

In the future I want to be a gunsmith and a gun collector and live in the country up in Alaska or Canada on a homestead where the land is free by myself with pet animals. I'd get up in the morning and go outside to the shooting range and shoot all day. Then I will go out and shoot some animals to eat the next day. Then probably*

(* The rewrite ended here.)

Rich entered kindergarten with a different haircut, rhythm, and language than the English 10 kids. By the "standard measurements" he was already "way behind." Right from the start the school gave catching him up a shot: remedial math and reading, special help with a migrant tutor, school breakfasts. But he only made slight gains. And he was absent a lot.

And the system's still trying to meet Rich's needs, to help him be successful, to offer him the chance to finish with a high school diploma. Rich takes Law and Security classes at BOCES in the morning (the closest any of the programs get to "guns"). In the afternoon he takes ILS, Global Studies, and resource room. He is classified LD (learning disabled) in written expression, basic reading skills (decoding) and math calculation. According to his overall CAT (California Achievement Test) score, Rich reads at a 6.0 GL (sixth grade reading level). Because he's not working toward a local diploma (regular), he does not have to take the RCT's (Regents Competency Tests) in reading, writing, science, and social studies. Rather Rich has an IEP

(Individualized-Educational Plan), which is a yearly-adjusted set of goals with alternate learning provisions that must be met in order for him to receive credit for that year, and at the end of 12th grade, an IEP diploma. The special learning provisions in Rich's IEP say that all his exams must be given to him orally and that he can use a calculator during math tests. Rich's IEP stipulates he must attend school 80% of the time to receive credit. 80% = 36 absences permitted. Rich was out 36 days last year.

However, all the acronyms poured into Rich's foundation still have not managed to bring Rich up to "grade level." The special programs, modified requirements, and extra help have not worked for many of the students in ILS. That is, they have not moved significantly beyond what the "standard measures" predicted for them when they started kindergarten. In terms of functioning in the "modern world" reality, Rich is still "way behind."

Perhaps part of this failure is because no matter how "hands on" and modified the programs become, much of school remains alien to kids like Rich. Certain values and assumptions underpin the structure of the system. Get good grades and you'll get ahead in the world. Keep a neat notebook and wear clean clothes and you'll learn certain roles that will get you at least neutral treatment when you have to take your child to the emergency room and when you step up to register your car at the motor vehicle counter. The medium is indeed the message, and the message often turns out to be true: Walk into an insurance office looking lower class and the agent is going to ask you if you're sure your check is good. In the event that you even have a checking account.

Why is it that most of the students in English 10 are middle class and most of the students in ILS are not? It's a complicated issue. But the fact that we are a society with deep class divisions is an important part of the answer.

Perhaps another reason for the lack of academic success with students like Rich has to do with expectations and self-fulfilling prophecies. In our attempts to meet some students' needs we expect less. Recent studies show that when schools institute higher standards, demand more rigor, many students make gains. Higher expectations result in greater achievement. The trick is how to set it up so that each person is challenged to his/her absolute limit on an individual basis, especially in at least one area that he/she feels a passion for. How might Rich's love of guns and his connection to the land have been used to form the core of his program almost from the beginning as he learned to read, write, measure, and analyze? Surely it's not the content that matters so much as a strong desire to know and from that growing fire to learn to be a self-starter, disciplined in all things; realizing that learning itself is inherently valuable and an important component to having a vital life. And that no area of learning, no vocation, is inherently more deserving of dignity and respect than another.

    I think about class and expectations as they impact the ILS program, when it comes to working with such students as Jerry and Calvin and Robert and Rich. Clearly these are students we haven't helped gain full entry into a language system. We've all seen and heard about those programs and teachers where tremendous over time (and overtime) energy have been given to a specific group and many of the students have unlocked, where children have been snatched from the patterns predicted by their language development upon entry. That some "disadvantaged" groups can make the leap proves that it can be done. Stand Up and Deliver. If we had been able to focus on Rich in a pre-school program and kept the adrenaline on full force for the next thirteen years, what would have been his options?

    Whatever the findings, the fact now is that Rich's life is in the woods along with the rest of his clan. And it may indeed be a good life. But it would be better if it was only one of his options. A choice. Maybe he'll get together enough money to put a trailer up on his relatives' land and between one thing and another, he'll make a go of it. But for sure Rich is counting the days until he's sixteen. And beneath Rich's sleepy exterior, he isn't so passive: There's a lot of Us and Them anger. As there is in most of the ILS students.

    One day I found the following free writing in with the rest of my papers. My guess is it was one of Rich's Letter to Self entries turned in by mistake, not something he would normally have shown me:

I try to stay out of trobly but I get into trubly for a lot of

> things in school that I don't do But the people here are fucking assholes this school out to be closs down the bus drivers are thefs They build stock cars there they work on their own cars. They alto be put in jail for ripping off tax payers and lose the jobs over all of this

Whatever the underlying causes, Rich continues to be absent often, an average of five or six days a month. He complains of back pain: scoliosis. He is gone when Chief Broom hurls the fountain through the asylum window to make his escape, gone when Lenny breaks Curly's wife's neck. He misses the part where Billy Budd strikes Claggart because he cannot unlock the truth from his stammering words. For Rich, school is a dream, made up of disparate fragments that never quite make sense. The only day-after-day moments he's fully here are when he and Neal jostle before the class begins.

Spring

19
Love

It's Monday, after an Easter Vacation without one nice day—rainy and raw—when what we'd all needed to gear up for the final quarter were hours in the sun, bike rides, softball games, and long walks along the railroad tracks. All my morning classes are grim and I don't have the buoyancy to lift them. Even Dale Henderson in English 12, usually to be counted on to give us a boost, is down, down, down. Spent the whole vacation fighting with his girlfriend, he tells us. Neither of them trusts the other to be faithful when he goes off to college. Dale's girlfriend is a slender, blond fourteen year old named Renee Jacobs. Dale and Renee have been going together for two years. Her locker is just outside my room so I sometimes pass the two of them there. Many mornings I have seen them staring intensely, fiercely, into each other's eyes. I always turn away and feel strangely uneasy.

Love.

In fact I am about to start working with Dale's girlfriend, Renee, 8th periods. Her math teacher and soccer coach, Gary Fine, approached me with pleas to help her with her reading just before vacation. Her ninth grade English teacher is only here mornings and that doesn't fit with Renee's study hall schedule. I wanted to say no, think of some excuse, since that is the only planning/correction time I have left now that I work with Cindy on her history 5th periods, but Gary is hard to refuse, one of those teachers who puts a lot of energy into pulling up kids at crucial moments. Yes, yes, I told him, but today when I think of working with Renee, it feels like just one more thing to do.

And I'm not looking forward to 6B. My plan was to have the class begin listening to *The Glass Menagerie* Wednesday, after the drug and alcohol counselor does an introductory session on families tomorrow. The counselor is a young woman who works out of the county chemical dependency clinic. She's available to talk to students individually every Tuesday and Thursday afternoon, but so far very few kids are stopping by to see her. She told the faculty that it might help if she could come to various classes and do some kind of non-threatening presentation. That would give the students a chance to check her out and know what she had to offer.

She and I did a trial run of The Glass Menagerie unit with my first period ILS group a few weeks ago. Using masks for the students to hold up, the counselor talked with them about various roles members of a family often play in trying to cope with living with an addicted person: superwoman, scapegoat, lost child. Then over four periods we listened to the sound track from *The Glass Menagerie* movie, with Montgomery Clift as Tom, and Julie Harris as his lame sister. It was like eavesdropping through the walls on the private struggles of a troubled family.

The first period kids connected with the conflicts, sometimes calling out with emotional responses, usually when their irritation with the controlling mother could not be borne in silence any longer. Afterwards we discussed the characters in terms of the roles presented by the counselor and many wrote journals about ways their own family tried to cope with problems. The first period responses were positive. Since these students showed a better understanding of family dynamics, we thought we'd try the same thing with the more difficult 6B. I had hoped to outline the ideas for them today and get some interest going by having them write a few paragraphs describing how they thought an ideal family would treat each other.

But now as I survey their grouchy faces and the slump of their bodies, talking about problems of abuse and dependency does not seem like the best way to cheer them up. Once again the lesson plan that looked fine on paper yesterday in the quiet of my kitchen is simply not going to fly in 310's weather today.

"What did you do over the break?" I ask them. Maybe a gripe session will lift some of the weight. Open a hole to push the unit through.

"Nothing."

"Watched television."

"Went to the mall."

"Fought with my mother."

"Slept."

Neal outlines an activity far enough under his breath that I don't have to hear it.

Jerry appears to be sleeping right now. Vic is back to reading the newspaper, only the top of his dark head showing above the headline. Lori has a bottle of black fingernail polish uncapped before her and she is just starting to do her nails. Robert is holding his nose in protest. Even Joe seems depressed. In fact, we all have that pale, seedy look of prolonged fresh air deprivation.

Trying to introduce *The Glass Menagerie* unit in such an atmosphere could result in shoving it into a such a dark pit that I might not be able to dig it out tomorrow, so I reach for my folder of sure-fire stories—stories that can save the day in almost any situation: Raold Dahl's "The Hitchhiker," "The Landlady," "The Ratcatcher"; Poe's "Tell Tale Heart," Mary Hood's "How Far She Went," Farley Mowat's "Walk Well, My Brother". . ., but unfortunately in the three years that some of this crew has been dug in before me, I've already saved the day with most of these. Then I come to T. Coraghessan Boyle's "Greasy Lake." Ahhh this should do it.

"Greasy Lake": a cautionary tale of a nineteen year old who on one of his first bored summer nights home from college almost kills a bad character with a tire iron in self-defense, and then, in flight from that, comes face to face with a dead body floating in the lake. Enough suspense, violence, gore, and jazz for almost every 6B taste. And by a stretch, we can tie it into the counselor's presentation tomorrow.

"Sit back and rest," I tell them. "Because of the weather conditions" —they turn to see the drizzle of gray rain—"I'm going to read you a good story."

> There was a time when courtesy and winning ways went out of style, when it was good to be bad, when you cultivated decadence like a taste. We were all dangerous characters then. We wore torn-up leather jackets, slouched around with toothpicks in our mouths, sniffed glue and ether and what somebody claimed was cocaine. When we wheeled our parents' whining station wagons out into the street, we left a patch of rubber half a block long. We drank gin and grape juice, Tango, Thunderbird, and Bali Hai. We were nineteen We were bad. We read Andre Gide and struck elaborate poses to show that we didn't give a shit about anything. At

>	night, we went up to Greasy Lake. . . .

In the final minutes of the period, their mood much improved, I say, "Ms. Brinner is going to come to class tomorrow."

"Who the heck's Miss Brinner?" Stan wants to know.

Before I can tell him, Joe says, "You know, that woman with the long black hair. The drug lady."

"The one with the green eyes?" Jerry asks.

"Yes," Joe says.

The bell rings. Many of their faces have a look of general interest.

Well, that may make a large enough opening to slide *The Glass Menagerie* through. Ms. Brinner's hair and eyes, an anticipatory set I didn't anticipate when I made up the plans yesterday.

By eighth period the drizzle has turned to icy snow. April. Our sixth month of winter. I see Renee Jacobs hovering uncertainly outside my door. I wave to her, but she doesn't respond. How different she is from her older sister, Jean. Jean, so solid in space. What is it Gary Fine said? Sometimes Renee just isn't quite . . . there.

"Come on in," I call to her from my chair where I have temporarily collapsed. I pull a student desk around and motion for her to sit.

"The weather," I say, as a kind of apology for my despondency.

"What?" she asks. Up close *her* eyes are a dreamy blue. Her shiny blond hair pulled away from her pretty, scrubbed face by two pink plastic barrettes. Child and woman.

"I'm feeling depressed by the rain," I explain.

"Oh," she says and slides into the seat.

We talk about how I might help her with her reading. Her English 9 class has just started doing parts of *The Odyssey*. We decide the best thing for me to do is talk to her ninth grade teacher to find out what would be most helpful.

Just as I'm about to give Renee a pass to go back to her study hall for today, with the hope of knocking off a set of reading quizzes, she pulls a folder from her loose-leaf and opens it up.

"Do you think you could help with this?" she says.

She places before me a handmade book. The cover is bright pink, with the title *Mr. & Mrs. Bear's Baby* printed in green magic marker letters across the top. Beneath that, is a picture of a very pregnant bear in a red polka dotted maternity top.

"This is for my Home Ec childcare project," she says. "And I just need someone to quick check my spelling before I trace over the pencil with markers."

As I turn the pages of this sweet little book, with its carefully colored pictures of the Bear family's tranquil domestic life, I'm trying to match this girl beside me, with the fierce creature whose locked-look into Dale Henderson's eyes is so intensely sexual.

20
Lori

Lori was out three days in a row. I was surprised to see how much I missed her thorny presence, and I realized how much her absence affected the class. Without thinking about it I had counted on her energy to help keep *The Glass Menagerie* going. I figured she'd have plenty to say about the mother, that her usual side comments would help stir everybody up. I'd hoped her interest, along with Joan's, would counterbalance some of the boys' uneasiness with such emotional material.

I was in this process of wondering what was up with Lori when Marie called me at the beginning of 8th to say that Lori was coming into school to pick up her back assignments.

"She's wound up about something," Marie said. "When I called this morning to see about her absence, she chatted my ear off. Downright cheerful. Not like herself at all."

What would make Lori so exuberant? I had a pretty good idea.

I think I may be pregnant.

Two years ago, the first time I came upon these words in Lori's journal, I stopped her on her way out of class: Have you talked to your mother? Do you want to talk to the school nurse? Do you want to come and talk to me? How are you feeling about this? Throughout my rush of concern, she just smiled and said she was okay; she wanted to wait; that she really wasn't sure yet. A few days later I wrote a note in the margin of her journal: Come in any lunch period if you feel the need. Her response, underlined and darkened, I'm fine. Several times in class I caught her eye and cocked my head: Are you all right? Again, a smile.

I saw no changes in her: still dressed in tight jeans and T-shirts, still the same blue eye shadow and pink lip gloss, silver fingernails. Still the same "watch out" manner with the boys near her desk. At the end of the second week, Lori handed me a folded letter on her way out: *I'm not. Luv, Lori.* The "o" in "not" contained a sad face, the mouth turned down, the eyes weeping tiny tears.

That night I sat down and wrote her a letter. I said that when I was in junior high I used to daydream about being pregnant. Not so much actually taking care of a baby, but just about me wearing maternity tops with little violets on them and me walking around with a glowing look on my face. I said maybe this was because I was an only child without any knowledge of the realities of little brothers and sisters. Then I told her about becoming pregnant when I was doing my student teaching and about how hard it had been for me to get up in the night to take care of a baby. How tough it was to be responsible for an infant along with substitute teaching and waitressing because we needed the money to help pay the rent and buy food. That I felt having a baby had added a lot of pressure to the beginning of my marriage. I felt it would have been better for me to have waited until I'd had more experience out in the world before I tried to build a relationship with someone else. That even at twenty-four I had not been ready to be a good parent. I saw Lori reading my note during Journal time. As she left the class, her only comment was, You waited until you were that old to have a kid?

Lori reminded me of several girls I'd worked with over the years, other girls who longed to have babies. Once I asked one of them why she wanted a baby so much. Because a baby will be all mine, she said. Someone I can love and who will always love me back.

Last year Lori started going with a boy from another high school, a boy who had already fathered a daughter. Sometimes the boy had the little girl for the weekend and Lori helped take care of her. From time to time Lori wrote little accounts of the baby in her free writing. For a few days Lori's boyfriend was in my regular senior class after a feud with his family who farmed in a neighboring district. He was a football-player, handsome, and during the short period he was in the class, his work showed good skills and understanding.

Last spring Lori wrote about going to the prom with this boyfriend, about the place they went to dinner, about the motel where they spent the night. She said they were going to get married as soon as she graduated next year. Lori was taking the BOCES cosmetology course. She said she wanted to open a shop in her home someday.

Just before the close of last year Lori once again wrote in her journal that she thought she was pregnant. Like all the girls in ILS, Lori was fiercely opposed to abortion. I asked her what was her plan if she had a baby. She said her mother would take care of it while she finished high school.

One night a few years ago when I was chaperoning a school dance, I noticed an attractive girl with yellow ribbons in her long hair, standing in the doorway, moving to AC-DC while she scanned the crowd in the darkened gym. At first I thought she was a guest from another high school, but then I realized she was a little older than that. I asked if I could help her. She said yes, she was looking for her daughter, Lori Sanders.

When Lori returned to school this fall, I saw that she was not pregnant after all. Who knows, maybe she would make it through to graduation with the first stage of her cosmetology work done.

Just before the end of 8th while Renee was finishing her guide sheets, Lori burst in. She said her boyfriend was waiting in the truck. Though Lori and Renee didn't speak, I had the sense they knew each other. I gave Lori the *Menagerie* tapes to listen to at home and went over what she needed to do to catch up. She kept glancing at Renee.

"I want to tell you something," she said, looking at the clock. Only a few minutes until the bell. She took a seat and drummed her nails on the desk until the bell rang and Renee was gone.

"I do not like that girl," Lori said.

"Oh." I turned one of the desks around and sat across from her and with that, her face changed.

"Guess what?" she said.

"I think I can guess. You are going to have a baby."

"How did you know?"

I laughed and asked when she was due.

"August. But I'm going to graduate."

Within a few weeks Lori went from looking like a high school girl to looking pregnant, wearing large shirts that say things like "Baby" with an arrow pointing to her rotund belly. She became quieter in class. The group treated her with deference as she sat with her feet propped up on the seat in front. She said she was having trouble with swelling.

Then she was out again for a few days. She called me during lunch time. The doctor said she had to go to bed and stay there or she might lose the baby. The school was going to provide her with a tutor and would I get the work ready for her each week? She said she still hoped to graduate even though she couldn't complete the cosmetology course. She told me to print everything on her disk to read and count toward her writing credit. I did, and this letter became part of her portfolio:

> *When you called you said something about me coming out for xmas, I said I don't think so. That's because I really don't see the reason for you to be seeing me. You left me when I was a baby and you didn't bother trying to see me grow up. You still can't remember the the day I was born or know what grade I am now. You don't bother to write to me or call and talk to me. Why should I try? I hate what you did to us. You beat mom, and I will never forget that you didn't try to get in touch with me since you left. You don't even bother to pay child support right. You pay $45 or $43 every two weeks instead of every week like you're supposed to. I have lots of expenses. I just started cosmetology and my kit costs $75.00 and I have to buy three smock tops at $10.00 each and a pair of white shoes at $20.00. That's a lot of money and I need it. Mom is trying her best and Lillian is giving me her cans and bottles. The money has to be in Monday. If I ever did come out to visit, I would not work in the barn or anything like that. I will not be treated like last time when I came up to visit. I want to be treated fairly with the respect I deserve. You made me-now you should do your part and support me. Well, that is the way I feel And I know the way you feel. You'll just deny it all like you usually do.*

Each week the tutor turned in a little less work. I called and encouraged Lori, but she said she felt lousy a lot of the time. In May the tutor delivered this note:

> *I have decided to try for my GED in the fall after the baby is born. Thank you for all your help. The test shows it's a girl. We're going to name her Catherine. I'll bring her in for you to see her when she's old enough.*
>
> Love,
>
> Lori

21
Vic

Whenever I gave an assignment, Vic Gantz's first questions were always adverbial in nature: How much? To what degree? and Why? They all meant: How little can I do and still get in the 80s? Because he had moved to Florida the middle of last year and then ended up not going to school, he was having to double up on his English classes. He took ILS 6B and English 10 seventh period. He was brimming with righteous indignation about this. First of all, it was stupid for him to have to take English at all. He could already read and write as well as he needed to for where he was headed. Then to have to take it twice in one year and with the same teacher was really a bummer.

Fortunately for us both, Vic usually could balance just this side of contentious. His tone was not threatening. Sparring with him was good practice. I needed work on remembering that students have the right to question the process, the right to be given explanations. In this, Vic was my teacher: He would never let me get away with an implied "because I said so."

Vic Gantz's academic performance would make good data for discussing the complexities of institutionalizing the "higher expectations—greater achievement" philosophy. Though he has resisted learning and putting forth more than bottom-line effort for the last eleven years of his education, he's a master at "working the system." He has honed his critical skills on cutting through what he sees as BS; he is sharp. When we saw a film in class, he usually psyched out what themes I was drawn to and then argued convincingly for another way of looking at it.

Vic absolutely would not buy the idea that because he was potentially a capable English student, I could expect more from him in ILS than I could some of the other kids. In English 10 where there were many outstanding students who worked hard and excelled, he pushed just enough to bring in 80s. If in ILS most people were being asked to write about a page or read five pages, he would not do one word more. I tried to convince him it was to his advantage to read good books like Tim O'Brien's *If I Die in the Combat Zone*, Tobias Wolff's *This Boy's Life,* or Farley Mowat's *Never Cry Wolf* rather than S.E. Hinton. My hope was that in the first page or two the strong voice of the narrator would startle him into sticking around to hear more. No, he insisted on reading the shortest, easiest thing he could get away with, and if I tried to require more, he argued until he wore me down.

Reading transitional teenage stories further reinforced his contention that I was wasting his time. And his time was valuable. Vic was living with the family of another boy in the English 10 class and he was supporting himself by working at a garage after school and weekends. He said he had a lot to do in his real life so he had the right to choose to do the minimum in school. He was also not above trying to use books done in English classes previous years or attempting to get by on the movie version. I always tried to call him on that: you may do less, but you may not cheat. He gave me grudging respect for being smarter than he'd originally thought.

I came to accept that in ILS, Vic would operate on one level and in English 10, he'd turn on the increased concentration it took to achieve 80% in a more rigorous program. It was a badge of honor with him never to give his all to either one of these stupid classes.

By chance I knew a little more about Vic's family than was the usual case. Nancy, a friend of mine, worked for social services in another county. One of her jobs was to visit families, to help parents better deal with their children at home and to show them how to work with their kids on skills needed for school. One day Nancy and I were at Friendly's getting ice cream when we ran into a woman and her adolescent daughter. It was clear there was a real bond of warmth between my friend and these people. I think because it was a success story, after we left, Nancy told me a little, without mentioning names. The woman had felt trapped in a destructive life of poverty out in the country on welfare with no way out. After several visits, Nancy became aware that the woman seemed very intelligent, and particularly able in math. With support, and getting connected to various agencies, the woman was able to complete college, and she was working as an accountant in a large city. She had two children. The girl was living with her and doing well, but the boy had chosen to stay with his father, and they were all concerned about him. It was only through some fluke later that I realized this woman was Vic's mother. I never mentioned it to him since I knew that he had very conflicted feelings about his family, particularly his mother, and that he would consider it none of my business.

Right from the beginning of the year Vic had made it clear that he would do best, and my life with him in the class would be much more pleasant, if I was willing to negotiate about some assignments, especially those that he considered invasions of his privacy. We began learning this process of bargaining back in October when I asked the students in English 10 to do Map interviews and personal narrative writing.

Because so many students find it difficult to image—to make movies in their minds—when they read and write, we often began the year with a first person novel or memoir that is rich in voice and image in order to practice and model "making mind-movies." In 6B we used *Cool World* and in English 10 we often started with *To Kill A Mockingbird*. As soon as we finish *Mockingbird*, the students make "maps" of some territory of their lives.

First I hand out a copy of one of my "maps" (12 x18) to each student. In one corner it says My Territory 1954 to 1957 and then the rest of the paper is covered with graffiti like writing at all sorts of angles: "feeling cold knees," "virginity tests at Charlie's," "Huntington, I've got a bone to pick with you!," "shoes in oven," "Vincentian boys & hickies" and dozens more. The words bunch up on top of little rough squares and shapes that say things like School, Boulevard Cafeteria, Apartment, Palace Theater, Casselaro's. I ask the students to guess what this piece of paper is. After a little study someone realizes it's a "map" of my memories of when I was in high school. Then I ask students to mark three or four phrases/words that have sparked their curiosity. Finally we go around the room and each student asks me to tell the "story" behind one phrase/image that interests them; which I do.

For homework, students are asked to think of one of the territories of their lives where they have rich sensory associations. The next day in class they make a "map" of that place and time. By sitting with a piece of paper and going to a specific place in your mind (up in your grandfather's hay mow, down by the tracks behind the trailer, in the closet of your bedroom) and in a particular time (when you were seven, when you were in Mr. Dory's fifth grade) your imaging mind activates and you will recall little wonderful incidents and particulars that contain the electricity that fires the bests stories and writing. Often, especially with adults, these are images that surprise you, things you haven't thought about since then. You try to systematically walk around your territory in your head, revisiting each of the rooms, alleys, street corners, trees where you spent time. Each time a person, place, incident, object, bit of something surfaces in your mind, you scribble down a word or phrase that will fix that memory as raw material for later writing and/or telling, usually labeling the place where you are and approaching the paper as though you have an aerial view of your whole little world of that period. All during the activity students smile and spontaneously share funny little bits that come to them.

The next day students volunteer to tell their stories from their maps at the rate of two or three volunteers in any given period. All the interviewer does is pick a topic from the person's map which leads to a spontaneous recounting of what's behind that image/word. The storytellers can exercise whatever level of control they want on what and how much gets said by having a friend or the teacher be the only one who picks maps topics. Or they can work from a set of pre-chosen images, or they can just let their maps go up and down several rows, letting kids choose a map topic of interest, with always the right to "pass" on any image/story they wish not to talk about.

As each kid tells his/her stories, several people are assigned to jot down on 8 x 14 paper, in large magic marker letters, the most electric image phrase they hear. We stick these "image posters" with phrases like "tied the muffler on with red and green fluorescent shoelaces," "flushed toilet and her hair went down," "spread his "cheeks" and pulled the BBs out with tweezers," "a goober leaked down his face and hung from his lip" on the strips above the blackboards.

Each map "interview" lasts about ten to fifteen minutes. In addition to the interviews the unit usually includes the students writing short memoir pieces: dialogues, descriptions of people, places, objects, and retelling of incidents using the maps as a source (or any other memories that come), and the reading of short first-person stories such as "The Kitten" from Richard Wright's *Black Boy*. Always the emphasis is on the use of images to "make the movie" for your readers/listeners in order to take them "there."

As I presented this map idea to English 10 back in October, I could see that Vic looked more and more disturbed—the scowl, the turning away of his body. Closing down. So I was not surprised when he came up at the end of the class.

"I'm not doing it," he said.

"Oh," I responded, beginning to work on that tension that had started to tighten my I Am the Teacher midsection. "Which part are you objecting to?"

"I'm not doing any of it."

"The map?"

"I'm not doing the map."

"The interview?"

"I'm definitely not doing that."

"The writing?"

"I'll write, but I'm not writing about my life. Why are we doing this stupid stuff anyway?"

I kept my voice even and explained again about the imaging. He listened like a lawyer, looking for a hole in my reasoning.

When he didn't rebut, I pressed on with a question that would prove if he was just being obstinate. "How about the short story reading?"

"I'll do that. I don't much like the stuff you pick out, but I'll do the reading."

"All right," I said. "When can you come in to work out an alternate plan that will achieve most of the same objectives?"

"I'm busy," he told me. "I work after school."

"Lunch tomorrow?" I countered.

"I'm not coming in here on my lunch break."

"Up to you," I told him, starting to get set up for what I had to do next. "But without an alternate plan and assignments, you're going to be collecting some zeroes."

He thought that over.

"Today after school for fifteen minutes," he said.

At 2:55 Vic was at my desk. For each part of the unit that he resisted, he had me explain the objectives again. As a substitution for the mapping, he agreed he would tell, with diagrams on the board, how various parts of the car work together to produce power. In place of the personal narrative writing he would do description, dialogue, action, but he'd either make it up or he'd base it on things that were not personal or close to him. I agreed. He had me write it all out and left at 3:10.

We started the interviews several days later and, as is usually the case with that activity, there was wonderful energy in the room. Even kids who usually feel frightened to speak in front of groups were letting go. There was a lot of laughter as kids popped us with image after image from their childhood memories. Since most of the kids had known each other since kindergarten, they were familiar with each other's territories, often showing up as characters in each other's stories. Sometimes even retelling or elaborating on the same incidents from their point of view.

In spite of himself I could see Vic enjoying listening. He was scheduled to do his talk next. I saw him busy scrawling something at the beginning of the period. When Vic's turn came, I was just going to say something introductory about him choosing an alternative, when he rose, kind of waved my remarks aside and passed out his scrawled list of phrases. He took his place on the stool, his dark head tilted to one side, his big hands draped confidently over the edge of the podium. We went up and down the rows and Vic responded with the stories he'd chosen to tell.

At the end of class as I handed him my evaluation, mostly just listing the image words that grabbed me, I said, "You did a good job with that."

"Figured it was easier than trying to explain an engine," he said and left.

A few weeks ago the English 10 class started the same Letter to Self unit that we'd done earlier in 6B ILS. Vic was wild at the thought that he would have to do that garbage again. He and I did work out enough variations to allow some of his steam to dissipate. Beyond asking how long did it have to be, he asked did the writing have to be true? I told him that was strictly up to him, that the project had only to meet the criteria of having energy, with evidence of having been really worked on and carefully edited, in addition to some guidelines for "quantity."

As agreed upon in his alternate contract, the beginning of last week Vic turned in a rough draft of a story as part of his project. Ideally this draft would have already been critiqued with a partner or writing group and then I would confer individually once the student had gone as far as he/she could with revision, and with luck, while the student still felt open to questions and comments to spur further rewriting. Since Vic's English 10 class had twenty-eight students in it, I often did the critiquing at home and then elaborated and clarified on a catch-as-catch-can basis when I returned the papers.

That night as I wearily went over the English 10 drafts that needed critiques, I started to read through Vic's narration of a drunken party thrown by a father and son, as seen through the adolescent boy's eyes. I began to feel the excitement a teacher experiences when, after slogging along through pretty bland stuff, Whamo, you come to a powerful story. One that, with some careful revision and fine-tuning, could actually "work."

I had two simultaneous reactions on what I needed to consider as I approached commenting on Vic's story: 1) How sad it was to hear the distant voice of this young narrator so early exposed to such darkness. His chilling inventories of drugs and women on hand. Numb. Jaded. I thought of my two sons, and I brought my concerns as a mother to the difficulty of growing up during a time when so many are spiritually adrift and the consequent use of drugs and other people to alter that void. Did I want to in some way make mention of this as I responded and, if I decided to speak as one human to another, how to do that without in any way shaming Vic? And 2) Should I mess with the story at all? I thought of Raymond Carver's work. I felt the writer of this party story, unknowingly, had chosen the "right" distance and voice to let us enter the darkness of that world. Much of the story's power lies in what is not said or consciously felt by the boy—the tension between the narrator's unreliability and the reader's awareness of what is beneath the surface becomes what the story is "about." And my gut feeling was that the writer of this story had no control over that, in no way had that been his intention. My guess was that this story was a somewhat exaggerated accounting of a party in his life and that it was chosen partly as a way to make me choke on my words that he could write about "anything." And partly to shock me (a mother-type) and to thrust his chin forward under a guise of fiction (if I should call him on it) to say, This is how me and my father live and I dare you to judge it.

All of this compounded by the fact that it was Vic Gantz's story so some "head games" on both our parts were inevitable if I made any suggestions at all. Finally, needing to get on with the stack of work ahead of me, I decided to treat this first draft with the respect it deserved as a potentially fine piece of writing, to spend my main energy on telling what worked for me and what I felt might be improved with revision.

First, I treated the work as a piece of fiction, immediately separating the writer and the narrator. Then I praised how clearly the writer had the narrator tell about the party and that the reader was interested from beginning to end. I said his including the morning after and the no-show of the social services "inspectors" worked for me. I commended Vic on the amount of effort (but not too much because heaven forbid I should make it look like I thought that he'd given it his all).

I also corrected his few remaining errors, though it was clear he had taken the time to already go over it with someone, which I thought was probably fun since I could imagine that they were laughing and saying, Wait until she reads this (words like cunt and pussy). I also thought that Vic's, "Ha, little does she know most of this really happened," might give some room for him to entertain the possibility of doing a little rewriting. I was careful to make the suggestions in the form of questions.

From a "good writing" point of view the description of the sex section was the only part that I felt really kicked the reader out of the story. The tone changed there and instead of that distant factual voice, I felt we heard the writer wanting to shock the reader, specifically me, The Teacher. That section just took over and became too boldly lit. The description of Loni and what the narrator did to her made her sound like "meat," and the boy's telling was so frigid and objectified, that I could not continue to grant the narrator sympathy. This was tricky because such comments could so easily feel like censorship. I attached a note:

> How about reading over the sex scene again. Does it sound completely real to you as a reader? Do you think the boy in the story would really have said all that? How does he feel about this woman? Does he feel any warmth or pleasure? You can leave it as it is if you're still satisfied after you reread it to yourself. However, if it doesn't ring completely "true," you might try softening it by cutting it down a little and changing any of the words that don't seem honest for what this boy was really feeling and thinking.

The rest of the story I mostly just went through and put pluses where I thought the image, voice, structure particularly worked, where I as the reader felt those little electric jabs. I also said that I felt the story had real potential to be published if he was interested in working on it further and that I had some stories by a writer named Raymond Carver about similar worlds that he might want to borrow. I added a P.S. in which I said that as a mother of two sons, I couldn't help feeling concern for the boy in the story; that tough things in our family, specifically the suicide of my sons' father when they were only eleven and thirteen, had made growing up very difficult for them, that indeed it could be rough "out there."

As I handed back Vic's draft the next day, I said I thought it was a good story and didn't need a lot of work to have him end up doing well on the overall project. I hoped this reassurance would ease his mind long enough for him to be open to my written comments. Out of the corner of my eye I checked from time to time to see if I could read any of his body language. He did look over my comments. But I couldn't tell anything about what he was thinking.

In a week, a few days late, which was enough to have him lose

I'm Sick of This Already

5 points off of his overall 90 for the project, he turned in the final draft. Unfortunately he did not also return the original draft which was always required so I could look at what and how the student had revised, and so he would understand that this evolving process really mattered, that rewriting was not to be just neat recopying, but instead a re-seeing and re-hearing. I give the main energy to the early drafts; for it is usually only during the rewriting process that I can help the student re-enter the piece, to learn strategies of revision (tightening, showing instead of telling, hearing how the sound and sense go together, etc.). Once most students have labeled a piece "Final Copy," closure has taken place, and much further critiquing is not productive. Best then to just praise the strengths and wait until the next project.

I read the final copy of Vic's story with particular interest, wondering if he had used any of the suggestions, and yes, curious to see if he had softened the sex scene to make it more in keeping with the tone of the rest of the story:

Vic Gantz   *April 23*
English 10   *Final Copy-Story**

It was Friday afternoon at about 3:30. Me & dad were on our way to the store to pick up food and beer. We had already gotten liquor for that night's party. While at the store we got a box of chicken halves and 10 cases of Michelob dark. Once we returned home, I got the barbecue lit. When the coals were good and hot I started the first batch of chicken. By now it was 6:00 and Bill and Rita showed up. They began to bullshit with my dad when I went inside to put the beer in the fridge, then took inventory on what was left in liquor. I thought to myself we got 2 bottles of Jim Beam, 1 bottle of Sambuka, 2 1/2 of Royal Crown, 1 bottle of vodka, 2 bottles 151 Bacardi rum and 1/2 bottle of peach schnapps. I went into my bedroom and got the rest of my stash out but there was only about a two finger bag left. I decided that wasn't enough to last the night. So I decided that I should scav-

enge the plants for more buds, but as I was on my way into the end room where the plants were dad hollered at me, "I already got a quarter pound. I don't think we need any more now." Okay I thought, as I turned around and shut the door behind me.

Midnight rolled around and the party was beginning to get wild. Mitch had come up with half a dozen women and Loni showed up. She brought some weed and a pint of rum. A bunch of my dad's friends came - some I knew; others I didn't. I was beginning to have some fun when we heard sirens and a cop car pulled in the driveway. I flipped. I was the only minor and I had a buzz going from weed and was staggering from Jim Beam and Budweiser. I grabbed the bag and the bong and headed for the house. At the same time all the other people were putting away their pipes and stuff. About 10 minutes later the cops left. Loni came into the house. She turned the radio down and came over to me. She said the cops received a complaint because of the loud music. Me and Loni took a few tokes on the bong, bullshitted a little and we went back outside. After getting stoned with her, I had gotten the munchies. I pigged out on chicken. I went into the house to take a piss, but when I got to the bathroom Loni was on her way in. She handed me the rum with about 3/4 of the bottle still there. Then she went into the bathroom I began to sip the rum. By the time she came out, 10 minutes or so, I had downed the whole bottle. Me and her talked for a few minutes when she just reached over and gave me a kiss. I noticed we were just about into the bag and after the rum I just drank I'd be plastered I knew so I began to caress her breasts in one hand and her ass in the other and we kept on kissing. I then removed her shirt . . .*

I woke up the next morning with my head pounding. I went to the kitchen and I grabbed 1/2 a dozen Tyle-

> *nol and a Michelob. I sat down on the nearest seat and thought about the night before. I didn't get too far into the thought when I decided that I better hurry to the bathroom and get ready to puke. When I finished with the dry heaves I returned to the kitchen to see my dad sitting there with an aggravated look on his face. He said that we have to clean the house up for tomorrow because the HRS people were coming to see if it was fit for me to live with my dad. It seemed someone at school complained. Then he said that he lost his teeth in the toilet while puking that morning and flushed it before realizing it. My dad got four of his bottom teeth knocked out in a fight, so he had a replacement set made. They locked around his other teeth. So I spent the day cleaning the lawn up, bagging away garbage and getting rid of both while dad cleaned the house. It seemed to be a joke anyway because HRS never showed.*

In the section marked with an asterisk * where the narrator begins to caress Loni and then fades out with an ellipsis . . ., the original version had several more paragraphs of details where the narrator tells what he did with Loni on the way to finally entering her.

I was sorry Vic had chosen the . . . fade out instead of really reworking that section, but of course I was not at all surprised. Vic *would* have the last word.

22
Jerry

Jerry knows how to take everything up to the edge; how to stop just before his front tires drop over. He enters class exactly between the click of the clock and my starting to make the "T" by his name. If there's been a big meeting on the wearing of hats and *all* that it signifies in terms of this country's imminent fall, he knows just how long and just how often he can wear his.

At the beginning of last year's Improvement of Language Skills class, Jerry's every move sent out little homing devices that bleeped me until they found a crack in my robot-calm. And always with a smile, his long legs sprawled in the aisle. Who me?

During his first few weeks in ILS, it was hard to know what Jerry could do because he would not read and he would not write. He was sixteen, but that was his first year of being mainstreamed into a "regular" English class. Since sixth grade his English time had been scheduled in the resource room.

At the start of the period, the first thing Jerry did, once he got to his seat, was to slip the handouts I'd put on his desk into his class folder so that he never had in front of him what he needed. When I'd direct the class to look at the top of the first page, he'd say, "What page?" I'd sigh and reach into his folder and pull out the sheets; then he'd glance at them and say, "This is dumb."

For the first week this ploy never failed. "Jerry, if you would just ... (blah, blah, blah)," I'd say. But soon Jerry's entry and the missing papers and his comment and my disgusted "Jerry ..." became such a joke with the rest of the class, a few of them mimicking bits of our routine, that we both gave it up.

No matter what I proposed, Jerry told me, "I'm not doing it." Eventually I learned to take no notice of this challenge. But what to do with someone who appeared not to read or write at all? Whenever possible, I had him work with a partner—someone unperturbed like

Kathy or Joe.

When we did silent reading, I taped articles from *Field and Stream* and blew up the print for him to try to read along with while he listened on a walkman, but the reading level was too difficult for him to keep following the print. I sent him to our 5-12 library to see if he could track down something of interest that he could follow on tape. He located a series on animals: short, factual accounts on about a fourth grade reading level. The ideal would have been to get a student to record the books, but I never quite got those arrangements together. Before I recorded a section, I taped simple "listen for" questions (also printed on worksheets) that Jerry had to answer as he went along. Usually he stopped the player whenever he heard an answer. He learned how to use parts of the questions to form his answers, adding in a few of his own invented spellings at the end. *What are some calls that are used when hunting turkeys?* When hunting turkeys, the calls used are . . . This being able to copy the beginnings of the answers gave him the confidence to risk, a sort of sliding down a structured chute before he dropped into his own confused symbol system. It turned out that Jerry still had real trouble following the print, so after about five minutes into the silent reading time, he would just listen. However, doing the worksheets pushed him to focus and continually read and respond to the questions. And it also kept him quiet.

Once Jerry started to be able to do some of the assignments, his concentration and effort increased markedly. By the end of September last year he wrote his first free journal entry, with Kathy available for his frequent How do you spells:

> *I lik to go turkey huntng wit my dad*

Another ideal might have been to do a lot of individualized work in the ILS class, which usually averaged about twelve in size, but because so many of the students, for a variety of reasons, lacked independent work skills, it usually was more effective, and kinder to my neck muscles, to set up the same lesson for the entire group, and then to help each one find a way within that project.

A structure we returned to again and again was to once a week have everyone choose one section of his/her journal to pull out and "make better" as they rewrote. Usually this meant to "go in closer" and show a few minutes of the incident or to tell it in more detail. Next they revised and edited this short, rewritten piece by reading it out loud to a partner. Then I did the final corrections and they copied it over after we did "common problems" drill on the board.

None of this worked too well for Jerry because his daily journals were never more than a few bare, flat sentences. Sometimes I would pass out a list of ideas that students could choose from to write paragraphs. Jerry would polish off the entire list in a few days:

> *My hopes are that I baley a car this weekend.*
> *My fears is dieing and drownding.*
> *My dreams are to have a nice truck and get married and have two cinds.*
> *My dreams are to have a bass boat and go fishing.*
> *My problems are I can not theich of anything to writ.*
> *I dislike being in a clowsed spase.*

And sometimes he refused to do even these. Most of last year when I could get to it or when I could set up a partner and Jerry was willing, one of us would draw a topic out of him, something he felt expert in: making a lure, cleaning his gun, the best way to track deer. Then his partner would ask him questions and as he talked, the helper would write his answers down in a short paragraph. Then Jerry would read it back and copy it over.

This year Jerry started off using that same pattern, except that now he needed less "drawing out." It seemed like it was time to advance to another level. One day he said, "Only put down the big words." As he talked, using large print I listed the key, hard-to-spell words and phrases. Then he read these back to me. Next he turned these into sentences to form a paragraph, read that to me, and we made the corrections. Then he carefully copied the paragraph over:

> *autobody*
> *work on cars*
> *Chevelle*

> *sanding*
> *down to the metal*
> *wipe off*
> *put paper over windows*
> *masking tape*
> *next paint booth*
> *wear a mask*
> *spray*
>
> *Final Copy 10/22*
>
> *I take autobody work on cars at BOCES. I am working on a Chevelle. I have to sand it down to the metal, and then to put paper over all of the windows with masking tape. Next I move it into the paint booth. I wear a mask while I spray it.*

I usually favor heterogeneous grouping. However, when it comes to working with students who have severe language problems, I feel ambivalent. One of the advantages of the more homogeneous ILS program is the "being more able to go on from where we left off" and the "being able to appreciate the inch-by-inch progress" since the student can elect to be with the same teacher for three years. To a teacher who hadn't worked with Jerry the previous fall, the above paragraph would read very differently.

Jerry worked well with "frames." He got so he could generate longer pieces alone if he just had some "bridges" to get him from one place to the next and someone available to respond to his frequent need for "spellings":

> *My Autobiography*   *Final Copy 10/26*
>
> **My name is*** *Jerry Daniels. I am 17 years old.* **Let me tell you a little about** *what I look like. I am 5' 11" tall and have a slight build. I don't eat very regularly so I'm skinny right now and I don't look too healthy. I ware blue*

genes and T-srese.

I think you'll understand me a little better if I tell you about *my family. I have one sister. She is 22 yrers old. She lives in a trailer. She is married. My mom works at New Yrer Central. She works 5 days a week. My dad works in Grantsville. He tends bar and when he doesn't work he and I go hunting and fishing. We have lots of fun.*

I've gone through a lot of changes in my life. *When I was younger I was a trouble maker.* **One incident that will show you what I mean** *was when I was fifteen, I threw an apple and then I got in trouble by the principal. He said, Don't do it agaen.*

(* The bold phrases indicate the frame that was provided for those who wanted "bridges.")

Though we were doing periodic silent reading blocks for two to three weeks at a time, it was still hard for reading to be real for students like Jerry. In January I decided to try a Children's Literature unit. Our elementary librarian put together a collection of the fifty most read K-4 books: *Cat in the Hat, The Hungry Caterpillar*, The Narnia series, etc. I also took out a big stack from the public library, partly made up of books I had loved: The *Pokiest Little Puppy, The Three Little Pigs*, and my sons' favorite books: many Dr. Seuss, *Winnie the Pooh, Where the Sidewalk Ends, Charlotte's Web*. I lined up one hundred books in the chalk trays around two sides of the room and wondered what 6B's reaction would be. My morning classes noticed them and registered interest.

The first thing I did after 6B was seated was to ask them to list their favorite books from when they were little. Only two said they couldn't remember: Neal and Rich. The rest bent their heads and began to write them down, clearly caught up in the warmth of nostalgia. Then we went around the room with everyone telling his/

her most favorite of all. Jerry said, That one with the gigantic peach. Many agreed with him. One of their teachers had read them *James and the Giant Peach* in third grade. Miss King, Jerry said, the one with the long purple fingernails and the nice legs.

When I asked everyone to go up to the chalk trays and pick out a few books that looked like they'd be fun, Jerry was the first one out of his seat. He seemed eager to have a head start. He chose *Katie and the Big Snow* and with a recommendation from me, *Where the Sidewalk Ends*. We planned to spend part of the week silently reading as many books as possible, keeping a simple record of each book completed. At the end of the same period we'd have "read arounds," with people holding up one page and reading to us out loud. Three times a week I'd begin the period with a continuing longer book: The group voted for *James and the Giant Peach*, and Thursdays and Fridays we would write rough drafts of children's stories, poems, and easy-to-understand informational books. Then if all went well, they would choose a draft and we'd all go to the computer room to do some more experimenting with the Macs: to do graphics and color and varied type to make individual and/or collaborative books. Maybe we'd even, for those who wanted to, go into elementary classrooms to read their books out loud. No one said, No way.

Almost everyone was "into" the unit, especially Jerry. The silent reading times were peaceful, with occasionally someone quietly sharing a picture or good part with a neighbor across the way. Jerry really liked the Shel Silverstein because a poem was manageable in length. He liked the idea of copying his favorites in his journal, going over the words and reading with me. He even read a few to the class during "read around":

> Inside everybody's nose
> there lives a sharp-toothed snail.
> If you stick your finger in,
> he might bite off your nail.
> Stick it further up
> and he might bite your ring off.
> Stick it all the way
> and he might bite the whole darn thing off.

Neal and Rich wanted to borrow the book immediately. Jerry said,

"When I'm finished with it."

The computer part of projects continued to prove very frustrating to Jerry—a whole new reading format. I told him if he could downshift and change a tire, he certainly could learn how to retrieve and save with a few days of practice, but he told me he felt like ripping out the keyboard and heaving it through the window. I sat him next to Cindy, who was purring along, and told her to signal me if she felt his frustration reaching the volcanic stage. Though Jerry never got beyond searching for one key at a time, and he lost more than he saved, still he did come up with several nursery rhyme variations that delighted him:

> *Fishie, fishie in the pond*
> *Daddey caught him with a rod*
> *Mommy cooked him in a pot*
> *And baby said, "He is so hot."*
>
> *Little Jack Horner stood on the corner*
> *Holding his big fat cigar*
> *He stuck it in his mouth, struck a match*
> *And said, "All I need now is a car."*

Jerry informed me one day that he was doing some reading on the BOCES bus, a half hour ride to and from his vocational classes each day. The autobody teacher gave out an automotive newspaper from time to time, and Jerry said he was practicing on that. He said he was reading about what coyotes eat, that he had figured out the word "grass." He said he didn't know a lot of the words, but sometimes it made sense. I told him to remember he didn't have to know all the words, but if he wanted to, he could circle the ones he couldn't figure out and bring them in and we'd go over them. He didn't ever take me up on that. Maybe he wanted the bus reading to be his, the real off-by-yourself kind.

In early spring Jerry had bronchitis and he was out for a week. When he returned, I told him he needed to come in during his resource room time in order to make up some of the work he had missed. This period corresponded to my planning period and no other students were coming in that day. I had for a long time wanted to work alone with Jerry, without ten other things going on in the room at the same time, to try to get more of a bead on how and why his language system was so off the track.

I asked him if he had any idea when and how his problems with reading started?

He told me no. Then he said, "Well, maybe it had to do with moving."

"Moving?"

"We moved nine times between kindergarten and third grade."

"Indeed," I said, "I think that might have had a lot to do with it."

I asked him to write a journal to make up for some that he had missed and to try to do it without any help from me, just to see where he was at this point, that I'd help him with it later when he started the rewrite.

He thought it over. Then he sprawled out and smiled. He put his baseball hat on and turned it around backwards.

"I can think better with it on," he said.

I said, "By all means."

He worked away for about five minutes:

> *My dad and I went turkey huning this morning. We saw a tom. but I didn't get a shoot. We saw some more way of in the feld. They flew up. It was fun.*

He handed me his paper.

"You should have been there," he said. "There's nothing like the woods early in the morning. The sun's just beginning to come down through the trees. That yellow-green just about to burst into leaves. There's mist coming up out of the valley. Everything below is hidden by the fog. We sit waiting. Way off there's the call of a thrush. Then quiet. All I can hear is my heart."

Ending

23
Lost

At the end of fourth period as the tenth graders are leaving, I notice the sun is out. Sun. I open one of the big windows and lean into those warm rays and breathe. Ahhh. Spring at last. The smell of mud. Mr. Dory has his fifth graders on the front field measuring distances with yardsticks. What could I do outside with 6B today that would so engage them they wouldn't lob pine cones at each other? But maybe Renee and I can do her Shakespeare work out on the front steps eighth period. I think with relief that it is the Capulets and Montagues Renee and I will be dealing with because a few days ago Renee showed me a story about teenage love that she'd written for English that is so dark, so full of jealousy and sex and lost children that I haven't had the strength or heart to do anything more with it. All I could say was that her writing had a lot of energy and that she had really made me feel for her characters. I did not say that the dialogue and images are still in my head, troubling and sad, and is it possible that you at fourteen have been in such worlds? I think about why *Romeo and Juliet* and "Greasy Lake," both in many ways similar in content, are so different; how with metaphor, rhythm of language and clarity of particulars, the nineteen-year-old's experience is filtered through some transformative energy. Art. With Renee's story, I take the easy out of helping her to correct her punctuation and spelling and leave the rest to her English teacher. Renee is always willing, but I never feel like she's quite "here." Right in the middle of reading or going over something, her attention dims.

As I start to lower the window a little, I glance down three stories and see a bunch of paperbacks and a red dictionary sprawled on the ground. Yes, warm weather has come at last. I do hope they're not from my room. If they are, I have to catch the hurlers at it and prosecute or dozens of 310's books will be jettisoned. Bad for the books and bad for my image with the custodians.

I'm Sick of This Already

I glance at the clock. If I quick set up for 6B I can walk up to the little school and back before the bell. In 6B we're getting to know the newspaper (again) this week. I push the desks into pairs: Neal and Rich, Joan and Stan, Jerry and Vic, Calvin and Robert and give each pair a copy of today's newspaper with a set of today's treasure hunt questions: What is the weather forecast for tomorrow? What position does the editorial take on the new bar closing hours in Marwick? How much is the Trans Am going for? What are the merchants on Dietz Street upset about? . . . The team that has the most points by the end of the week gets a pizza and everyone who completes at least half the questions gets a soda. So far Vic and Jerry are ahead.

I'm just going to dash outside when Marie stops at my door. I'm about to burst forth with some celebratory remark about spring, when the look on her face freezes me to a halt.

"What, Marie? What's happened?"

She scans my empty room. "There's an emergency meeting in the library," she says and without any further explanation goes on to free another teacher.

I hurry to the library. I know something terrible has happened.

The room is full of teachers. For a second I wonder how it has been arranged to have so many of us there at once.

Our principal, Jeff Larkin, is standing by the door; Frank Davis, the superintendent, beside him. I find a seat and he begins. Gone any trace of his usual jocular manner.

He looks at us for a minute. His eyes are full of tears. He breathes and then he speaks. "Dale Henderson is dead."

There is a wave of shock. The murmur of how, when?

There is the relief of hearing the worst and finding it is some distance from me.

Again someone asks what happened.

Jeff tells us that his death occurred this morning before school, that the police are investigating.

Several voices ask again was it some kind of accident?

Jeff says that's about as much information as the investigators want him to discuss at this point.

Something criminal. Suicide? I reject this as not possible. It's true Dale was not in English 12. His name was on the absence list. Then I think of Renee. I want to ask, Does Renee know? Has someone taken care of Renee?

Mostly we are stunned.

I hear Jeff's words and take in what I need, but the sounds are muted, the room dimmed. He says he has very little information for us at this time, he must tell us enough so that in a few minutes when we return to our classes and he makes an announcement over the public address system, we will be a little more prepared to deal with the students' responses.

I look at the clock. Twenty-five minutes more of fifth period. I want them to go ahead and make the announcement soon so there will still be no students in my room. I do not want to deal with any responses.

I want to go home.

We are told that all kinds of rumors will be going around, but that it's hoped we will simply stay with the official PA announcement: that Dale is dead; that no more information is available now, pending further investigation. Students will not be permitted to go downtown or home for lunch today. Everyone will eat in the cafeteria. All of Dale's teammates are right now meeting with the coaches down in Gary Fine's room. Someone asks about Renee and the superintendent says Reverend Bernard took her home earlier in the morning.

The library and Will Booker's room will be open for students to talk to local ministers and counselors from several area schools and agencies who are just beginning to arrive. Students are to report to their classes for attendance first. Teachers should give passes to anyone who needs to talk. There will be another brief meeting at the end of the day to set up plans for tomorrow.

Many teachers are crying. People hurry back to their classes for the announcement. They comfort each other as they go.

I speak to no one. I go to my room and turn off the lights. The announcement is made. I unpair the desks and collect the treasure hunt questions and newspapers. I sit and wait for 6B to arrive.

The bell rings, but the halls are strangely quiet as students pass to their next classes.

Only Calvin, Robert, Rich, and Joan report to 6B. Mr. Booker sends up a note saying that Joe is with him. I call Marie and report

I'm Sick of This Already

Stan and Vic missing. I ask the students present if they want to talk. They shake their heads. Jerry and Rich sit on the back table and look out the window the rest of the period. Joan puts her head down across her arms. Calvin folds his hands in front of him and seems to look at nothing. Robert turns the pages of a magazine. I sit at my desk and study the student murals, the energy and care in the work.

At the end of the period as they quietly get up to go, Joan says, "I think it's true what they're saying."

My look answers, Please don't tell me.

I stay in my room for lunch. Most of my seventh period tenth grade class signs out for the library or Mr. Booker's. I offer no comfort or wise words to anyone. Special bulletins are given out to all classes eighth period for each student to take home to their parents or guardians.

After the buses have gone, the PA announces the meeting for all staff. I do not go. Teachers are gathered together in small groups outside the library. I pass them and drive home. I don't watch television or read a paper. I know tomorrow will be soon enough to know what I have to know.

The next morning I arrive early. I close my door and open all the windows. Already it is bright and warm. A few sixth grade boys are throwing a ball on the lawn below the terraces. One laughs and punches the pocket of his big glove while he waits. If I could go through the day without seeing anyone else, I would. At eight o'clock someone knocks on my door. It's Gary Fine.

"You weren't at the meeting after school," he says.

"No."

"How much have you heard?"

"Nothing."

"Ginnah, you need to know this now. Renee was arrested yesterday afternoon and charged with second degree murder."

It is Friday. Then it will be Saturday and Sunday.

"She was arraigned last night and sent to Renfield Juvenile Detention Home in Utica."

"All right," I say, meaning that is enough.

He nods and stands up, but does not leave.

"Are we to give passes to the students who want them?" I ask.

"Just like yesterday. There will be a candlelight vigil here tonight. And no school Monday so people can go to the funeral." Finally he turns to go. Then he comes back and really looks at me, but all he says is, "I hope you and Sally will put together some books for her."

Most of the students sign out to go to Mr. Booker's or the library. Many students are absent. The students who stay are quiet. They put their heads down or look out the window or do their math. Or they sit in pairs up and down the hall, talking softly, crying, hugging. Kathy comes to tell me that the seniors are with a counselor in Gary Fine's room.

"How are you doing?" she asks.

I tell her that I am getting through the day. She says her sister was afraid to walk home yesterday, that she had to get Mrs. Baker to drive them.

Many of the kids in 6B are on the absence list: Joe and Joan and Neal and Rich. Calvin and Robert and Jerry sit and look at the newspapers.

A girl's voice in the hall says, "We should kill her. That bitch."

I close the door and call to report Stan and Vic missing.

Then I take Dale Henderson's folder and his high school cumulative writing file from the box. I place them in my drawer. They need to go to someone. Who would Dale want that to be?

Piece by piece Renee's story surfaces in the newspapers. How at 3 a.m., a few days before Dale's death, she and her sister found Dale hiding in the bedroom closet of another girl. How in revenge Renee went to another boy's house after school. How Dale discovered this and in dozens of phone calls he told her to get it through her head, it was all over. How early the next morning Renee wrote him a letter, one of three hundred letters they had exchanged in the last two years.

> *You should not be mad at me cause you did the same thing to me. I can't believe all of this has gone wrong. I really need to shape up a little. And I guess you do too. I really want a relationship now. I can really make this work as long as you don't cheat on me. But I didn't do anything on you lately. I wouldn't cause I realized you*

> mean a lot to me. I know I mean something to you too. If you didn't care you would have broken up with me a long time ago and wouldn't of cared what I think or how I felt. Well all I can say is I love you.
>
> *Me Forever*

The papers tell how she called her friend before school to say that if she could not have Dale, no one else would. How she put the letter and a kitchen knife in her backpack. How Dale picked her up in his mother's car and they drove to the river, to a place they'd often gone. How, as they stood by the car, she asked him to please hold her one last time and how he refused. How she gave him the letter and as he read it, she stabbed him in the chest. It was determined that this first wound to his heart was the cause of death, but when he fell forward to the ground, she stabbed him again and again and again.

The building is quiet. Everyone has gone for the day. I reread some of Dale's journals, getting ready to give them to someone. I read again the words he wrote one month ago:

> *I dream alot about this girl that I think is everything. Whenever I see her she stops everything around me just by looking at me with her beautiful eyes and smile. I would give everything to be with her forever & to make a family with her. I tell her all the time how much I love her. I just don't know how she feels about me. There is nothing wrong with her in my mind when I hold her & kiss her. I never want to let go, ever. Words can't express how I feel. I just hope someday she'll know.*

I think of Dale. Renee. Dale's mother. I cry, cry for us all.

24
Balancing

Mid-May and finally the newspaper headlines are no longer about Dale and Renee. After threatening phone calls, Renee's family has left town and gone to live in another part of the state. Gary Fine is in touch with them and with Renee. Renee is being held in a detention center, having been denied bail several times. She will be tried in criminal court sometime this summer, with talk that if she should be convicted, she might receive a sentence of from eight years to life. Her lawyers' attempts to move her case to family court have been denied. The key themes seem to be her rage in repeatedly stabbing Dale and the prosecutor's continued claim that she has shown little remorse. The many photographs of her taken at hearings and being led handcuffed from here to there by state police show a young girl in a white hooded sweatshirt. Her face pale and lifeless, eyes blank. Anesthetized.

I hear from Renee's sister, Jean. Jean makes no direct mention of what has happened, but she says she often reads the words of Andre Dubus that I sent in one of my cards to her, that she finds them comforting:

> After the dead have been buried, and the maimed have left the hospital and started their new lives, after the physical pain of grief has become with time, a permanent wound in the soul, a sorrow that will last as long as the body does, after the horrors become nightmares and sudden daylight memories, then comes the transcendent and common bond of human suffering, and with that comes forgiveness, and with forgiveness comes love.
>
> from *Broken Vessels*

There is less angry talk against Renee; there is less talk about what happened. People have started to go on with their lives: beginning to think about finals, graduation plans, going off to college. Almost everyone in 6B has written a few journals about what happened. There was a lot we didn't know about Dale; there was a lot we didn't know about Renee, Joan wrote. She said she could understand somebody loving someone so much that they might want to kill them. Neal said, Even the big shot kids have problems just like in *The Outsiders*. Joe wrote poems and stories about times he and Dale coon hunted, but he didn't show these to us, didn't leave them in his folder. Calvin said that he didn't feel safe in Stanton anymore, that it was getting to be as dangerous as a big city. Stan wrote that Renee should get the electric chair. Jerry said he couldn't understand why anyone would want to do something so dumb. Robert wrote that it was a sin. Rich and Vic remained silent.

A few weeks ago, on her way from the BOCES bus to the library, Joan stopped in. Her blue-red hair a little wild, her glasses a little askew. She looked disturbed.
 "Good to see you back," I said. She'd been out for a few days.
 "My daughter was sick, but she's okay now."
 I was about to ask about her daughter, but Joan charged on, "Hey, how come our class didn't do *Romeo and Juliet?*" She'd noticed the English 9 students walking around with the book. One of them told her all about it at lunch yesterday. "It isn't exactly like what happened, but in some ways it is. Romeo and Juliet were crazy in love too."
 "Yes, I can see your point," I said. I had thought Sally Burton, the English 9 teacher, brave to be able to go on with the play in Renee's class. She said it gave them a safe way to talk about their fears. Love. Death. Families.
 "In fact, how come we never read half the stuff the other classes do?" Joan asked.
 I thought about this: why we hadn't done Shakespeare, Dickens, Twain.
 "I just don't think I could keep the class interested for the four or five weeks it would take to get through it," I told her.
 For me, this is one of the big problems of grouping all of the poorer readers together. If Joan (or any number of the ILS students) were in with the English 10 class, she would be exposed to these other worlds. The better readers in the regular curriculum create a momentum that pumps enough energy into the class to keep moving

forward day after day. With discussion and response journals and a kind of "playing around with the language" attitude, it's possible for students to stay connected enough to have a positive experience and take in the material on a lot of different levels. It gives everyone a chance to explore the big archetypes so helpful in coming to terms with the difficulties of being human.

But without that language power at the center of the group, all those hard words and all those pages can be just too intimidating. Even books like *The Yearling, To Kill a Mockingbird, This Boy's Life* have not been possible with ILS. Not only is the vocabulary and length daunting, but there is a real problem with tone and understanding that what isn't said is often what's most important. That what a character tells us may be unreliable. Some years we have struggled through *Bless the Beasts and Children* and *Never Cry Wolf* with me doing most of the reading, but even then Calvin and Robert and Jerry and Rich and Stan operate on the far edge of frustration, creating a restlessness in the classroom (daily choruses of complaint, calling out, sleeping, projectiles, desk graffiti, etc.) that is beyond my neck's tolerance.

True we have had good success with some fine films such as: *On the Waterfront, Awakening, In the Heat of the Night,* and even fair responses to a few audiotapes like the sound track of *The Glass Menagerie.*

I know there are teachers who, out of their deep love and knowledge of a subject or writer, are able to bring even their most needy students to a connection with the material. However, it is seldom that I've attempted to take an ILS class as a whole group on such a long journey through the labyrinths of the printed words of the more difficult texts.

But individually it is sometimes possible to get a little closer to the language and themes of more challenging literature. We decided to set Joan up to work on *Romeo and Juliet* independently. First, she read through the scene summaries in the Laurel Edition and we went over the parts of the plot she couldn't follow. Then she watched the film of the Zefferelli version on her own down in the library workroom. She said even though parts of it were very confusing, she liked it: the clothes, the furniture, the fights, the lovemaking. She thought

Romeo was cute, and she liked it that he seemed to love Juliet a lot more than she loved him. I asked her what had led her to this conclusion. She told me she could just feel it. She said it all made her understand Renee a little better. At this point she was ready to give the Elizabethan text a go. However, after a day of listening to the audiotape on the walkman and trying to follow along in the book, Joan said she'd had enough; she already knew they all died in the end. It ruined the suspense, she said. Maybe so, but her response journals already showed her learning to integrate and question her own experiences and Renee's in relation to this young couple, and she had the satisfaction of saying that she'd studied Shakespeare, which indeed she had.

Helping students who were motivated and who had more language development to combine text, film, and audio to work independently and in small groups did solve some of the problems of how to deliver some of the classics and more challenging literature to some of the students. Kathy had been enthusiastic about listening to the unabridged tapes of Amy Tan reading *The Kitchen God's Wife* and she completed all eighteen hours, sometimes following the text at the same time. But again this didn't work for everyone: Cindy gave up after the first side of tape one. Vic listened to *The Loneliness of the Long Distance Runner* with an intensity of focus far beyond his usual distance, actually taking side four to finish in his truck. (Though he turned off *The Picture of Dorian Gray* after fifteen minutes saying he couldn't get into that aristocratic BS.)

Of course there were a few classics that we could read. In March we successfully completed *Of Mice and Men* reading every other day as a play, with Vic consenting to do the third person narration, and a few others willing to regularly play the major characters: Joe as Lenny, Neal as George, and Joan as Curly's wife, with me taking the long dialogues of Candy, Crooks, and Curley as needed. Jerry slept and Rich was absent so much he was lost and Stan insisted on going to the bathroom during the final scene when George shoots Lenny so the end of his life is in the midst of his dream of rabbits, rather than in terror and humiliation at the hands of Curley and Carlson. I don't know if that was lack of interest or a way to avoid such an emotional scene. But everyone was present the entire week that it took us to watch the follow-up Malkovich-Sinise film. And even Jerry gave that a 5 for excellent, saying that though the guy who played Lenny didn't have big enough hands, he did do the talking right.

Earlier in the quarter we had another triumphant showing: *Billy Budd*, with a lively discussion at the end of justice vs. the law led by Joe who could see why the captain had to hang Billy and opposed by Stan who felt a mutiny was in order. Stan liked the film so much he borrowed the DVD to watch at home. When he finally brought it back days later, he recommended that everyone else in the class take it home too. He said he was still seeing new stuff even after the third time.

Feeling optimistic about such progress, I was just trying to track down a short, not too hard modern classic as a final end of the year unit when 6B once again lost its balance. Within one week four more students dropped from the group.

On Monday we learned that Joe ran away to North Carolina with Summer because her father slapped her in front of a bunch of people on Main Street. Mr. Booker had had contact with them on the phone. They were safe, living with relatives of Joe's, but for now had no plans to return before the end of school.

Neal didn't show up for class on Tuesday. It was unusual for Neal to be out. His name wasn't on the absence list. I asked did anyone know if he was in school? There were a lot of whispers and downcast looks. Joan said Neal was being accused of something so bad she could only tell it to me privately. I told them I didn't have the strength to hear any more bad news right then. Later in the day Joe Marsh informed me that Neal would not be returning before the end of the year and asked if I would prepare a final that he could take outside of school under supervision. Joan did not offer any further information and I did not ask.

On Wednesday Robert transferred to a special afternoon class at Grantsville Central. He just stayed on the BOCES bus and got off there. He didn't tell us goodbye. When I talked to his mother on the phone, she said yes, she knew it was late in the year, but he had a new job on a farm over there and she'd made arrangements for him to go to summer school, and this way he could get a head start on the workbooks. She didn't want to criticize, but it seemed to her all we did was watch movies, and she couldn't see how that was going to teach Robert how to read the difficult labels on the cows' medicine bottles. And in my present state of weakness, I thought there was a real possibility she might be right.

It felt a little as if we'd been speeding on cruise, with our seat belts off, when one of the doors had silently opened. By the time I'd looked back, half of the passengers had already been sucked into space. In the midst of all this and probably partly as a consequence, Stan went into a week of unparalleled belligerence and destruction: a fight in the room with Rich, the removal and loss of the insides of my telephone, the wreckage of the space bar on one of the Macs in the computer center. All compounded by his refusal to sit in an assigned place during silent reading or to leave the room to go to Mr. Booker's as a result of that refusal.

On Friday, I sat down with Joe Marsh and Will Booker, and we set it up for Stan to be given independent work the remaining two weeks. He would be placed at a carrel in direct view of Will in the "time out" room. I would conference with him briefly eighth periods to go over his assignments and he would be given an opportunity to read out loud with me for ten minutes each day as part of his credit. I lost the faith that I could contend with another stretch of Stan's negative behavior and help what was left of 6B to come back to calm and purpose. Dale Henderson's death, Joe's sudden departure, Neal's disturbing removal, the loss of Robert without a farewell had left us without much will to press on.

At the end of that week I stood at the podium and looked down the rows of empty desks. Then on beyond them to the single hemlock and the American flag moving slightly in the May air. Beyond that to the green hills of spring. I listened to the strange stillness of a school building after everyone is gone.

Then I updated the 6B chart, which though I had long ago stopped using it for seating arrangements, still contained the record of departures:

SEATING CHART — 6B (12:15 to 12:57)

Victor		~~Patty 12/6~~	~~Cindy 1/27~~		~~Lori 5/3~~
~~Kathy~~	~~Stan 5/21~~	Joan	~~Sam 9/8~~	~~Vance?~~	~~Robert 5/19~~
		Calvin	~~Beth 9/7~~	~~Joe 5/17~~	Jerry
~~Neal 5/18~~	Rich	~~Mike 2/7~~		~~Allen 10/2~~	
Row 1	Row 2	Row 3	Row 4	Row 5	Row 6

Out of the original seventeen, only five students remained: Vic, Joan, Jerry, Calvin, and Rich. The whole drive home I wondered: What would be a good plan for 6B's final two weeks? What would catch and hold all five? What could I have them do that would not necessitate my energy being at the center of the class, that would allow me to rest, for I felt very tired indeed? I was surprised when I found that my car had come to a halt in front of my house, twenty miles from room 310. I could not remember passing through the small towns en route, stopping for traffic lights, or making any of the required turns.

25
Ending Big

Lesson Plans — ILS 6B (9 day unit: 6/1 through 6/11)

Content: Great Expectations (Masterpc. Theater DVD)

Objectives/Rationale: 1. To continue to provide ILS rich, challenging material (similar to the regular English curriculum) in a form they can handle 2. To set up "in common" material for a collaborative 60 minute final exam (6/15) 3. To provide a wide range of data for final diagnostic evaluations of overall individual gains made in expository writing, critical thinking, discussion, and listening skills for the year.*

(* What I am going to tell Calvin's mother if she calls to ask why he has been watching a movie for nine days in a row.)

As I drive to school Tuesday morning, grateful for the Memorial Day reprieve, I am almost restored to the belief that we can make it through the remaining twelve days until school lets out for Regents. Mindful of the traffic lights, I construct a 6B scenario: Joan, Jerry, Vic, Rich, and Calvin will sit huddled before the TV, watching Pip discover that Joe Gargery, a simple blacksmith, is the true gentle man, and many other values worth thinking about, for three hundred minutes while I withdraw to my desk in the back of the room to rehabilitate and critique thirteen English 12/Government research papers and forty English 10 literature essay rough drafts.

By the end of fifth period, the room is June hot. The dark shades are pulled to within a foot of the ledge. There's a fan whirring on the back table in front of the open windows. The distant sound of sixth graders, playing softball on the lawn three stories below, laps at the edges.

The bell rings. I stand beside the TV Emma Lowe has just delivered and tested, leaving me with the injunction to guard it carefully. The DVD of *Great Expectations* has been fast forwarded to the title screen with its peaceful background overture ready to flash ON the moment I press PLAY. Focus guide sheets, headed with the words: *Watch this movie like a hawk. These are your FINAL EXAM questions,* have been placed on a small crescent of five desks, arranged at a perfect distance for optimal viewing.

6B appears, a wan skeleton of its former clamorous self.

"What's this?" Jerry says, his baseball cap angled low over his eyes.

"A television set. Duh!" Joan tells him.

"No, this?" he tells her, sticking a guide sheet in her face.

"A piece of paper. Duh!" she says, pushing the guide sheet away.

Calvin takes the seat on the left and opens his pencil box.

Rich sprawls beside him, stretching his legs so long they almost touch the guarded TV stand.

Vic sits on the right and moves his desk back two feet. I've already tracked him down in the hall earlier to tell him how much this DVD is going to help him with his *Great Expectations* (long unread for homework) English 10 Final Exam Essay (rough draft due Friday).

"God, where is everybody?" Joan asks, casting a lost look toward all the empty desks.

I decide to pass out the lollipops I'd planned for the final day. When I go by Jerry, I point to his hat which he pulls off almost simultaneously, as though the lifting of his hand is an answering echo to my gesture.

We go through the format for the next nine days and a brief overview of Pip's journey. We take turns reading the guide sheet questions: *(Be sure you can give specific details from the movie to support your ideas.) What are some similarities and differences between Dickens' world of the mid-1800s and your world now? What are some of the turning points in Pip's life and how does he change as a result of these? What are some of the things Pip has learned by the end of the movie? In what ways is Pip's growing up journey similar to yours? Different from yours? . . .*

Then their voices boil over with suspicion: "You mean we get to do the Final Exam together?" "That's cheating." "How come?" "Can we do it alone if we'd rather?"

I explain that it's to see how each of them does at working with the group, to see how they are able to build on each other's ideas in comparison to the beginning of the year. How these kinds of skills are very important "out there." I point toward the windows, toward the village that squats below. Calvin turns to see where I mean.

"Are we getting graded on this sharing stuff?" Vic wants to know.

I tell them mostly I'll just be evaluating their progress. The actual final exam grade we can agree on in individual conferences, but that their understanding of the movie is likely to be much greater if they pool their thinking.

Knowing how hard it is for most of them to get names and people connected, we go over the list of characters that is printed in large letters on the sheet. I suggest they put down a few words of description for each of the people as they meet him or her in the movie, some distinguishing physical image, that they can refer to in order to finally know who's who.

"Can we use it during the test?" "Can we look at our notes?" "Can we borrow the DVD to take home to look at again?"

Yes, yes, yes, I tell them.

I remind them that we will stop five minutes before the end of the period each day so that we can go over any parts they are finding confusing, to discuss any questions they might have. I remind them not to call out during the movie since that spoils the mood, a thing we've been working on all year.

I move to start the DVD. Joan turns off the lights.

"I suppose it's in black and white," Rich mutters.

The image emerges. Colors flash. They smile with satisfaction to see it is so modern. I stay for just a minute to adjust the volume. They lean forward, lollipop sticks protruding from their mouths. I tiptoe quietly back to the serenity of my desk as the movie opens on the marshes, with grown-up Pip standing by the skeleton of an old gallows, his "flashback" voice speaking to us over the distance of time:

> "Ours was the marsh country, down by the river, within twenty miles of the sea. My first vivid impression of things

177

I'm Sick of This Already

seemed to me to be gained on a memorable raw afternoon toward evening. At such a time I found out for certain that this bleak place was a church yard. I knew that the dark flat wilderness beyond was the marshes; and that the low leaden line beyond was the river; and that the distant savage lair was the sea, and that the small bundle . . ."

I am just settling into my chair, to day after day of quiet paper-critiquing, when it happens.

Jerry throws up his hands and turns to me in the darkness, "This friggen thing isn't even in English."

"Yeah!"

"Who the heck is that?"

"Where are they?"

"Who's the kid?"

"This is stupid."

The voices of ten year old Pip and the convict stream by underneath, unheard. So many clues to establishing the world of the story already lost.

The nine day carpet of freedom that had unfurled before me, rolls up, and I am once again buried in the belly of 6B.

"Hold on," I tell them, moving toward the front of the class. I press the STOP. "Don't panic. I hadn't realized it would be so confusing at first. Let's make an adjustment of plans. First let me get you a little grounded as to what's going on at the beginning of the movie. Then we'll start over and slowly, as things happen that you don't get, I'll kind of whisper enough information for you to reconnect."

Their bodies mostly relax. Vic is grinning at me.

"And maybe, Vic, you can help us out since you know a lot from us doing the book out loud 7th period. For some extra credit."

His face becomes neutral. Which I've come to believe means he's in there, looking over his hand.

I put the tape on rewind, with us watching the images streak by backwards. I explain that Pip is about thirty years old when we see him by the gallows, a place where they used to hang people, and he's looking back on his life and that from time to time, this older voice is going to speak to us, over the action on the screen. That the boy we see is Pip when he was about nine and he's going to be grabbed by a convict who's just escaped from a prison ship and that this event is going to turn out to be important. That the story is a mystery so there are a lot of things that we're just to register, but that won't make full sense to us until much later.

We decide it's worth putting down some identifying phrases for the characters we'll meet today, since if they do it while the DVD's going they'll miss things looking down to write in the dark: Pip: an orphan, 9 years old; Joe: Pip's sister's husband, a blacksmith, blond curls; Mrs. Joe: Pip's sister, about thirty, skinny with a mean mouth.

I remind them we'll only get about ten minutes into it before the end of the period. We breathe and start over. I sit next to Jerry because I figure he will have the most frustration and the most questions.

And that's what we do. Day after day the story of Pip unfolds before us. When Jerry and Calvin and even Rich quietly ask about who or what or when or why, Vic or I briefly give the small piece that's needed. Sometimes Vic tells them, We're not supposed to know that yet. Sometimes he says, We're just supposed to be questioning that and starting to have a theory.

At the beginning and end of the periods we go over identities and pin down clues and facts that are necessary to "getting" what will come later. Jerry gets good at supplying us with the identity tags: Miss Haversham: the crazy lady with the white hair; Estella: the bitchy girl with the cold face; Mr. Jaggers: the fat guy with the bushy eyebrows.

Soon it all gets easier to follow. There are fewer and fewer questions. The class is clearly into it, even Vic. From time to time he fills in his English 10 essay frame with notes. Jerry does not feign sleep. He censures Pip for being so "snotty" to Joe in London. Calvin is interested in the cobwebbed, darkened rooms which Miss Havisham hasn't left for twenty years. Joan is concerned about if she ever bathes and how she goes to the bathroom wearing that ragged old wedding dress. Rich says if Pip had stayed out in the country where he belonged, none of this would have happened. They like getting grossed out by the spiders and mice crawling around in Miss H's rotted wedding cake. And they all want to know, What does Pip see in that Estella anyway?

Just as the big rough man who has come to Pip's apartment late at night leans toward Pip and asks him if the name of his lawyer begins with the letter "J," Rich whispers, "That's the guy who was in the graveyard" and Joan leans toward my ear and says, "I bet five dollars he's who has been giving Pip the money. Not Miss H."

Toward the end of the period one day, Jerry begins to give off electricity. Finally he says softly to Vic, "Well, I've got a theory: That woman with the big wrists and the messy hair is Cold Face's mother."

After class as they're going out Joan asks Jerry how he figured that out.

"By the way the camera kept showing her hands when she was knitting," he tells her.

With only 25 minutes to go to finish the DVD the next day, we decide to have an end of movie party. People kick in money for Mountain Dew. Joan volunteers to make a big bag of popcorn. On Friday, soda and buttery bowls before us, we settle in for the final scenes: Pip going to the forge after Joe has cared for him in his illness; Pip asking Biddy to marry him and learning that she and Joe will wed that summer.

"Too late for you," Joan mutters.

We watch as Pip goes back for one last visit to Miss Havisham's house before they tear it down. We see him slowly going through the dark hall.

Jerry tells us, "You can hear by the music, she's going to be there."

"She's dead," Calvin says.

"Not the Crazy Lady. Cold Face," Jerry whispers.

Just then one of the boys in my English 12 class comes in. I motion to him to meet me at the back of the room to answer some question he has on his research paper. Though he speaks in a somewhat lowered voice, it is loud enough to be heard.

I'm about to suggest that he speak more softly when Jerry rises and backs quietly toward us. Still watching the screen, he says in an all-business undertone, "You think you two could go in the hall? We're just about to come to something big."

Epilogue

Two Years Later:

Mrs. Howard: (*the teacher, the one who was always deep breathing and rolling her neck*) Retired. In transition; volunteering at an elementary school several afternoons a week: reading to little kids two at a time in the hall, and helping four fourth-graders one-on-one with their reading. If she could come back in another life, it would be as a kindergarten teacher.

Calvin Brooks: (*the boy with the concerned mother; he always had his pencil case ready and liked to imagine future living spaces; one of the final five*) Still in school; getting along with everyone pretty well; hard worker—doing two part-time jobs; has a beat-up car, but it runs.

Robert Brooks: (*Calvin's brother; the boy who came back to work lunches and who wrote about rolling the Camel cigarettes in his T-shirt sleeve; transferred to another school just before the final weeks*) Received an Individualized Educational Plan (IEP) diploma from another high school in June; now a "migrant farm worker" doing milking and labor on different farms.

Vic Gantz: (the boy who had a 12th grade reading level; the one who wrote the story about the drunken party and who always wanted to know how the work would be graded; one of the final five) Vic and another boy were killed a few days before graduation when Vic's truck went over an embankment. The speedometer still registered 80 mph when they were found.

Joan Monroe: (*the girl who had a baby at fourteen; the one who worked on* Romeo and Juliet *independently; one of the final five*) Had another child; returned to school in the fall after being out for a while; felt she needed more education to get a job as an aide working with children with disabilities; completed her credits for an IEP diploma in December.

Rich Spencer: (*the boy who brought the beaver teeth to school; loved guns, one of the final five*) Left school in December, the day he turned sixteen; shot a ten pointer in November.

Joe Tyler: (*the boy who rolled the joint out of pencil shavings; ran away to North Carolina with his girlfriend, Summer, just a few weeks before the close of school*) Completed the BOCES program and graduated with an IEP diploma in June; living with his sister and her husband in North Carolina and working as a mechanic in a motorcycle shop.

Lori Smith: (*the girl who often wrote about becoming pregnant; wrote a letter to her father venting her anger about his treatment of the family; left school in May due to complications related to pregnancy*) Now has two children and living with their father.

Mike Burns: (*the boy who wore the latest fashions and almost never did a lick of work; had mono; transferred to English 10 class in February; had to repeat tenth grade the following year*) Still in high school; doing better with work and attitude because he has the goal of going on to school in Maryland as a mechanic.

Vance Jones: (*the boy who always wore his jacket and sunglasses; had a good class interview; almost never there*) Quit school officially in November; people who see him around town say he looks like he's having a rough time.

Stan Sadowski: (*the boy who squashed the bug the first day; a saboteur of VCRs and computers; watched* Billy Budd *several times at home; removed from class to work independently down in the time-*

out room the final few weeks of school) Still in school; is no longer belligerent; seems happy; has become an excellent welder, scoring third in a regional competition; working on putting together a portfolio of welding jobs; going for his tractor trailer license soon; very motivated in his government class, learning all of his lines for his role in a mock trial and appearing in a suit for the "day in court"; usually carrying an autobody magazine when seen in the halls.

Patty Morgan: (*the girl who camouflaged herself except for her bright red nails fluttering up in disgust; had two very different sisters; forgot her junior prom program in her folder; left school in January*) Her name was paged at the county fair (summer): Please call home immediately. An emergency.

Cindy Lane: (*the girl who wrote poison pen letters to Mrs. H. and said she'd be lost without her boyfriend; transferred to Independent English in January*) Eventually passed all of her Regents Competency Tests to receive a local diploma in January of that next year; working full time at the Victory Market; she and her high school boyfriend have ended their relationship.

Allen Lange: (*the red-headed boy who squealed his sneakers on the parquet; went to Florida and when he returned shot Calvin with a squirt gun; removed from ILS in October to be returned to a self-contained special class at BOCES*) Quit school the following fall, then returned to school for one day in September the next year; left the area.

Kathy Flanagan: (*the girl who was always asked to help; the one who listened to* The Kitchen God's Wife *and one day had the courage to say No; transferred to English 12 class January.*) Graduated with a local diploma in June; now working as an aide at a daycare center.

Neal Thomas: (*the boy who liked to make naughty asides; liked to sit at the podium; left under a veil of silence a few weeks before the close of school*) Accused (some say unjustly) by his sister of molesting one of her children; left the area.

Jerry Daniels: (*the boy who liked to turkey hunt with his father; had theories about* Great Expectations; *one of the final five*) Still in high school; restored his grandfather's car and did a beautiful job; is in charge of the evening shift at a local body shop.

Renee Jacobs: (*the girl who killed Dale Henderson*) In August, during a painful trial, experts for the defense stated that the hundreds of letters the couple wrote indicated that Dale Henderson was a manipulative person who had coercive power over his young, unstable girlfriend and that his many infidelities pushed her over the brink. The jury found Renee not responsible by reason of mental disease or defect. It was argued that she was going through a temporary psychosis. Renee Jacobs will serve no prison time; she is required to have out-patient counseling for five years. Many in the town, including the judge who sat on the case, were outraged by the verdict. Students and citizens, led by Dale Henderson's mother, organized several parades and rallies to protest the final outcome.

Acknowledgments

Always I am grateful for the comments of my West Kortright Centre and Cedar Key writing groups and the opportunity to read excerpts of this teacher-narrative during the open mike sessions at Word Thursdays in Treadwell, New York. My thanks for the gift of time without interruption granted to me by The MacDowell Colony, the Saltonstall Foundation, Blue Mountain Center, Ucross, and Hedgebrook. And finally kudos to Valerie Haynes, the founding editor of Illume Writers & Artists, and Jane Higgins, Illume's Book Designer.

Ginnah Howard's work has appeared in *Water~Stone Review, Permafrost, Portland Review, Descant 145, Eleven Eleven Journal, The Tusculum Review,* and elsewhere. Several stories have been nominated for a Pushcart Prize. Her novel, *Night Navigation* (Houghton Mifflin Harcourt 2009), was a *New York Times Book Review* Editors' Choice. *Doing Time Outside,* Howard's second novel, was published by Standing Stone Books in 2013. The final book of the trilogy, *Rope & Bone: A Novel in Stories*, was published by Illume in July, 2014. The National Alliance on Mental Illness of New York State gave Howard their Media Award for work on behalf of those with mental illness and their families. For more information visit: www.GinnahHoward.com

Made in the USA
Charleston, SC
03 November 2015